HEIDELBERG DAYS
1964–1968

Frank Lyons

Copyright © 2014 by Frank Lyons.

All rights reserved.

Heidelberg Days 1964–1968 is based on Frank Lyons' memory and research of events in West Germany where he lived from 1964 to 1968.

Book cover photo by Dreamstime LLC.

Heidelberg Days 1964–1968 is available for purchase from Amazon.

Manufactured in the United States of America.

The author may be contacted at fwlyons4@mchsi.com.

ISBN-13: 978-1505439830
ISBN-10: 1505439833

This book is dedicated to the most important people in it:

My late wife, Rita Lyons

My children, Kathleen and John

My wife, Jean Lyons, who helped me in countless ways
as I wrote *Heidelberg Days 1964–1968*

And in memory of my parents,
William Lyons and Mary (Donohoe) Lyons

CONTENTS

Preface	vii
Introduction	ix
Chapter 1 Moving to Germany	1
Chapter 2 Heidelberg	14
Chapter 3 Overseas Expansion	26
Chapter 4 Living in Germany	33
Chapter 5 The German People	55
Chapter 6 The Konrad Adenauer Era	65
Chapter 7 Building an Iron Foundry	81
Chapter 8 The Ludwig Erhard Era	94
Chapter 9 The Looming Bear to the East	102
Chapter 10 Postwar West Germany	117
Chapter 11 Postwar East Germany	129
Chapter 12 Postwar Nightmares	137
Chapter 13 Traveling in Europe	147
Chapter 14 Career Development	162
Chapter 15 Going Home	170
Chapter 16 What Came Next	182
Bibliography	194
Photographic Credits	196
Acknowledgements	198

PREFACE
How *Heidelberg Days 1964–1968* Came to Be

Since my second retirement—first from the John Deere company, a farm equipment manufacturer, and later from Emerald Associates Inc., a manufacturing consulting company—I have followed my lifelong passion for writing. It has become a dominating interest since I finished practicing my engineering profession. *Heidelberg Days* is my fourth book.

When I lived in Heidelberg, West Germany, with my young family for four years in the mid-1960s, it was a high adventure. But from the vantage point of a half century later, I now recognize that I occupied a ringside seat for witnessing and recording the next phase of the post–World War II transformation following the initial emergence from the rubble and chaos of the war. I decided that I had a story that should be written.

The entire population of Western Europe was still reconstituting itself with the hope that another devastating world war would never occur. This was carried out with the looming and threatening Russian bear to the east looking for any opportunity to foist her suffocating communist system onto the West.

Throughout the book, I used the commonly accepted term Russia. Before the collapse of communism in the late 1980s, the more correct name was The Union of Soviet Socialist Republics (USSR).

Heidelberg Days is an account of what I observed, heard, and read about during and after my tenure living in West Germany followed by a backward look five decades later when I wrote this book. I was compelled to write this account when I reflected on what a rich personal and historical time I had experienced. Writers of history often demonstrate Arnold Toynbee's claim, "History is just one damn thing after another." I tried to disprove Toynbee's implication that reading history books is a better way to go to sleep than counting sheep by humanizing and personalizing my account of the times. I told my story by showing a connection wherever possible between the history of the era and my living adventure in West Germany.

I wrote *Heidelberg Days* with the intent that it would appeal to readers of German history—particularly the legions of foreign soldiers and civilians who lived for a time in postwar West Germany. I also wrote with the hope that the book would be informative and amusing to armchair readers.

I was inspired by Mark Twain, who lived and wrote in Heidelberg a century earlier. He observed German culture through the eyes of an American as he wrote in his satirical style. We both were enabled to live and work in Germany by our employers: Twain was employed by a newspaper publisher and I worked for a farm machinery manufacturer.

I was guided by some of the writing techniques that helped Twain write in his clear, understandable style: He listed every word that could express an idea. Then he selected the simplest word from the list. He said, "The difference between the right word and the almost right word is the difference between lightning and a lightning bug." And he disliked "the fluffy adjective" habit. He advised, "When you catch an adjective, kill it."

Although I occasionally refer to and quote Mark Twain in *Heidelberg Days*, I do not have the slightest expectation that our respective readers will think we dipped our writing quills into the same ink well. When I compare Twain's talent to mine, I must resist the temptation to return my quill to the tail of goose that provided the feather.

INTRODUCTION

By the mid to late 1960s, the US and other NATO members warily faced Russia and her Warsaw Pact allies. They were like bulls snorting and pawing the earth ready to butt heads at the first sign of provocation. The US and Russia were the only still ascending world powers.

Although the initial phase of the postwar era was largely over, the consolidation of the vast changes continued. Germany was split into West Germany and East Germany. Each was established along vastly different and conflicting political lines. Russia was still in the process of establishing communism in her homeland and the Eastern European countries that she dominated, and the US was still consolidating her large military presence in Western Europe. The Cold War dominated the news of the day as if it were a weather report predicting a never-ending storm watch.

Officially West Germany was named the Federal Republic of Germany (FRG) and East Germany the German Democratic Republic (GDR). In this book I refer to them by their commonly used names, West Germany and East Germany.

The events recounted in *Heidelberg Days*—historical, personal, and professional—occurred primarily during the time I lived with my family in West Germany. But to broaden the perspective, I frequently drifted into the past and projected into the future.

Recollections from my boyhood in the US during World War II provided related information about the events described in this book. I further acquired information from a lifetime of reading history, biographies, and general interest books. I rounded out my research by reading a wide selection of the many available books written about wartime and postwar Germany. If there are factual errors, misquotes, or misinterpretations, I alone accept the fault.

Several events, from a different viewpoint, were recalled by my daughter, Kathy (Kathleen), from her girlhood in Germany. My son, John, was too young to have more than a few dim memories of his German boyhood. Unfortunately, Rita, my late wife and partner for more than thirty years, was not living to participate in the writing of *Heidelberg Days*.

The book speaks of the post–World War II era that directly and indirectly touched our lives. In the 1960s, powerful and vivid memories of wartime and postwar years still intensely occupied the minds of all Germans and most Americans. The people of both countries were still struggling with how to proceed in a dramatically changed world while the menacing—and sometimes oafish—Russian bear to the east tried to define and establish her role with her newly found power and influence. She was attempting simultaneously to develop and to spread the largely unfamiliar and unproven communist system—only several decades old—in her physically vast and culturally varied country and in her satellites.

Russia soon discovered she could not earn respect and acceptance for her suffocating, totalitarian form of communism as she inflicted it with an iron fist. But, she learned she was very good at scaring the stuffing out of people by dreaded midnight knocks followed by a ride to an interrogation center where confession would be extracted, by whatever means, for being a Trotskyite, a devisionist, a saboteur, a traitor or anti-party; then, if still living, on to the gallows, firing squad, or a Siberian labor camp. For groups of rioters or protestors there were lethal barrages of tank and artillery fired point-blank into crowded city squares.

One of the most effective means of Russian control in occupied Germany was food rationing. The best grade of rationing was reserved for those who cooperated most fully with the Russians; the worst grade was scarcely enough to sustain life.

Sullen and grudging submission by resisters to Russian demands always followed after the "persuasion methods" of fear, force, and famine were applied.

Russia's conduct at home and in Eastern Bloc countries recalled medieval times when gruesome bear-baiting matches were held. Virtually defenseless bears were declawed, defanged, and chained before they were set upon by bulldogs; the dogs never lost.

The initial conduct and leadership of the Western Allies in occupied Germany immediately after World War II was also nothing to write home about—but it was nothing like that of Russia. The Western Allies were like dogs chasing and catching cars and then not knowing what to do with them.

Many war-weary GIs went on a binge of postwar drinking and womanizing. German women were far more prevalent than men, and they were in desperate need of the necessities that GIs could provide from PXs. Relationships between GIs and German women were often free and open. Although at first there was a nonfraternization policy with the U.S military forces, it was largely ignored. After families were allowed to move to occupied Germany, the rambunctious behavior of GIs subsided.

Based on the initial poor behavior of the occupying Western Allies and the public revelation of the callous deals agreed to for the future boundaries of Europe by Roosevelt, Stalin, and Churchill, the Germans saw few reasons to view the Western Allies as benevolent conquerors although their opinion of them was much more favorable than it was of the Russians.

One of the most difficult challenges in writing *Heidelberg Days* was to square the multiple viewpoints on the culpability and accountability of the German people for their inhuman behavior toward the people Nazis despised—Jews, Jehovah's Witnesses, Gypsies, dissidents, handicapped people, gays, and Slavs—during the barbaric twelve-year reign of Hitler's Third Reich. At first—in my naivete—it seemed evident that all Germans should be scorned and clothed in sackcloth and ashes for the atrocities of the Nazis. But when I took the first step in that direction, the path immediately became twisted and uneven as it lead through a tortured landscape of guilt, hate, fear, denial, shame, atonement, defensiveness, confusion, contradiction, truth, lies, and suspicion. It quickly became obvious that all Germans should not be painted with the same brush.

Although I recalled the major events of World War II, in many instances I needed to learn more about the related details. For this, I referred to the books listed in the bibliography shown at the end of *Heidelberg Days* and, when possible, by talking to Germans and GIs with firsthand experiences during the war years and the aftermath.

However, I found out over the years that "firsthand" information was sometimes tainted. People from areas ravaged by war often had no documentation and had an urgent need to start new lives in new lands on the most advantageous terms: clerks became executives, technicians became engineers, nurses became doctors, barons became counts, Nazi criminals became streetcar conductors, and teachers acquired PhDs. Their stories were hard to confirm.

I recognize that interpretation of what I remember, analysis of available research material, and my personal observations sometimes differ from the strongly held viewpoints of others who were directly involved in the war or who are history scholars. They are entitled to their viewpoints, but I lean to the bias suggested by Churchill when he facetiously said, "History will be kind to me, for I intend to write it."

The differences between the US and Germany in physical terms were superficial when compared to the psychological differences.

My outlook came from an American world of security, prosperity, freedom, isolation, and victory in past wars—Revolutionary, Mexican-American, Civil, World War I, and World War II.

The outlook in postwar West Germany was influenced by her history of an oppressive, totalitarian government: the wicked conduct of the Nazis during the time of the Third Reich, massive forced population relocations, dire suffering during and after World War II, and her profoundly humiliating military defeat in two world wars. West Germany needed to regain her self-esteem and earn enough respect to be readmitted into the council chambers of the civilized nations.

Overlaying this turmoil was the continuing fundamental conflict between communism and government control in East Germany versus capitalism and freedom in West Germany. An epic contest was underway to determine if capitalism or communism would prevail. It was the time of the Cold War, a period that would persist and consume incalculable human and material resources for a half century.

All of this profoundly colored each person's perceptions of the postwar era. The dissimilarities of experiences and circumstances were too great for both sides to write the same history books.

As I tried to gain a balanced perspective on the volatile history of Germany during the turbulent postwar era, I had to overcome the drawback of speaking limited German, only reading background information written in English, and not having personally endured the agonizing wartime and postwar suffering of most Germans.

My professional life primarily involved engineering and manufacturing. But my private life involved interest in history, current public affairs, and diverse cultures. My interests were fed by reading newspapers, news magazines, history books, biographies of influential people, and selected fiction, as well as talking to diverse German people.

Although I became broadly informed, there are gaps in my knowledge. My familiarity with German and European culture, history, language, and customs is not always comprehensive. I am like an indiscriminate crow collecting baubles—my collection is also incomplete.

As I analyzed and wrote about postwar events in Germany, I did so with recognition that it is much easier to write from the vantage point of 20-20 hindsight while basking in the victor's winning circle. The predictions and expectations about the future shaped in postwar years did not line up with the new and vastly different world that would actually unfold during the next half century.

As I learned more about the war during its final days in late 1945, I decided that I could never grasp the horrors that went on in Germany and the countries to the east at that time. In many cases, it was even worse than the steady, more orderly dreadfulness earlier in the war. The killing frenzy and dying were too much for me to ever comprehend. It was a burden that could only be borne by those who experienced it, and it forever ruined the minds and lives of many.

The final phase of World War II was a time for: (1) the Red Army to vent its rage as it blindly pushed its way against the remaining German army and civilians; (2) the undersupplied, undertrained, and underfed German Army—mostly boys and old men—to senselessly fight until the last man; (3) foreign forced laborers to roam the country seeking food, clothing, and shelter—and sometimes revenge; (4) released prisoners from concentration camps to even the score. (5) rampant disease epidemics—especially typhoid—starvation, exposure, and joblessness; (6) bullying and lawlessness by German civilians who took advantage of the breakdown of the police and legal systems; and (7) relentless and pitiless bombing of defenseless cities.

Even Churchill challenged the severity of repetitious allied bombing when he asked, "What is the purpose of making the rubble bounce?"

The death rate during the violent, dreadful final phase of the fighting spiked to the highest level of the war.

If the closing battles of the war were made into a movie, the only theme music powerful enough for the film would have been Tchaikovsky's thundering "1812 Overture" written to commemorate Russia's expulsion of an earlier foreign invader, Napoleon's Army. The tumultuous final crescendo, accompanied by thundering cannon fire and brilliant fireworks, would characterize the final orgy of death of the once mighty German military and the merciless bombing and shelling of cities—followed by abrupt silence. And in the ensuing silence, the horrors would continue with millions more deaths by suicide, disease, starvation, and exposure.

I realized our blessing, as Americans, for not having to live in the miserable, disgusting mess left from the ravages of the war. We could pack up and go home to our intact and prosperous country.

In writing *Heidelberg Days* I linked my professional and personal life as much as possible with the teeming, ongoing developments in West and East Germany in the mid-1960s. It was a challenge to decide which events to include from the mountain of available material. I felt like a hungry animal jumping up on a banquet table and sniffing through the abundance of food offerings to select the most suitable to its need and taste. I concentrated on the more important events that either directly or indirectly impacted my life.

But maybe I deluded myself somewhat in the selection process for picking subjects to include. I probably was influenced by what personally interested me the most.

There was much omitted from my writing even though it had relevancy. For instance, the once mighty but now exhausted British Empire was still struggling to fly her Union Jack around the world even though it was a futile effort. In 1962 Dean Acheson, US Secretary of State, said, "Great Britain has lost an Empire and has not yet found a new role."

The same can be said of France. Her worldwide colonial empire was crumbling fast. Her humiliation was complete when she lost Vietnam and later Algeria. Eisenhower, who endured the arrogant attitude of the French during World War II, called them, "… a helpless, hopeless mass of protoplasm."

And there also were other important connecting events underway in France, Italy, Spain, Greece, Ireland, the Benelux countries, Scandinavia, and North Africa.

But to write of all of the events in these countries, even though they were relevant to postwar Germany, would necessitate following the model of migrating Monarch butterflies; it takes them three to four generations of time to travel to their destination.

Heidelberg Days is not intended to be a comprehensive history of West Germany during the 1960s. To write such a story would be far beyond my proficiency and too encyclopedic in scale for any single person to tackle. For generations, individuals and even entire institutions have devoted their talents to writing history books and novels about World War II and its aftermath, the postwar conflict between East Germany and West Germany, and the Cold War.

Readers who wish to learn more about that fast-moving and formative German and European postwar history can look to the books listed in the bibliography pages of *Heidelberg Days* as well as to the many new books being published based on the boundless trove of information recently made available from secret files of the Stasi (feared secret police of East Germany) and the KGB (terrifying state security police of Russia).

Books by Anne Applebaum and George Bailey are especially authoritative, informative, and readable. For a comprehensive historical look there is *Postwar, A History of Europe Since 1946* by Tony Judt. For readers of fiction, there are no better espionage thrillers than the John le Carré novels written about Cold War intrigue and espionage—especially his best seller, *The Spy Who Came in from the Cold*.

INTRODUCTION

There was seldom a richer time in history to live in and write about. Thomas Cahill, historian and author, aptly called such times, "The hinges of history."

The fertility of postwar German history recalls comparison to similar periods in the US. Streams of books are still being written about the eras of Abraham Lincoln and John Kennedy, who also presided during pivotal eras with great challenges and changes. For such times and such iconic figures, there are always new perspectives to consider from freshly discovered letters, notes, pictures, diaries, whiffs of scandals, secrets and—most important—from the added clarity possible when the writer knows how things finally turned out. The public is always ready to absorb more information about great events, especially when they are associated with colorful people like those who guided the new order of post–World War II.

I frequently quote other writers who express themselves better than I. I do not have the skill and the gall of George Bernard Shaw who boasted, "I often quote myself. It adds spice to my work."

Heidelberg Days is a story that has four interwoven strands: (1) my family's days living in Heidelberg; (2) the history-altering political and economic events of Germany and Europe from 1964 to 1968; (3) Russia and the Cold War; and (4) the business expansion of my employer, the John Deere company, into Europe. The strands all connected with the two worlds where my family and I existed—our secure and tranquil domestic realm and the turbulent and daunting world outside our door.

To understand the meaning of the events of the mid-1960s in Germany, it was necessary, in some instances, to follow the strands into the future. It was easy to follow them in this direction because I wrote the book a half century after the events occurred.

Most of the uncertainties and anxieties of the 1960s are now laid to rest. It is the behavior, motivation, and actions of the pre-1960s historical players (Hitler, Stalin, Churchill, Roosevelt, and Truman) that remain open for interpretation and explanation. This continues to be an insurmountable challenge even to the world's best psychologists.

Although much in the world changed in later decades, my family's close bonding, established during our years in Heidelberg, endured. During this period of our lives, we lived especially close within our own family distant from relatives and old friends.

The single most important aspect of my life was my personal relationship with Rita. Although our innermost communication was largely by nonverbal means, I hope the users of this book will be able to read between the lines and sense our mutual respect and affection. When we were together, we shared our private lives in a cocoon of exhilaration. I was in awe of her. Without Rita, I would not have been a whole person.

When we left Germany after four years to return home to the US, a nostalgic song by Mary Hopkin was popular; it captured our dreams and moods during our *Heidelberg Days:*

Those Were the Days

Those were the days my friend
We thought they'd never end
We'd sing and dance forever and a day
Those were the days
Oh, yes, those were the days.

CHAPTER 1

MOVING TO GERMANY

*Travel is fatal to prejudice, bigotry,
and narrow mindedness.*
—Mark Twain

*Travelling with children corresponds roughly to
travelling third-class in Bulgaria.*
—Robert Benchley

Lufthansa Plane Departing from Chicago

My wife, Rita, and I were 33 years old when we and our two young children boarded Lufthansa Airlines Flight 431 from Chicago O'Hare International Airport bound for Frankfurt Rhine-Main Airport in West Germany.

It was a few days after Christmas in December of 1963. Lanky, hard-driving Lyndon Johnson had recently become president of the US after the assassination of elegant, charismatic John Kennedy.

Portly, easygoing Ludwig Erhard had just become the second chancellor of postwar West Germany after fifteen years of political and diplomatic heavy lifting by his studious and austere predecessor, Konrad Adenauer, the George Washington of modern West Germany.

The "Happy Days Era" in the US following World War II was over. The New Frontier vision, as confidently and eloquently articulated by

John Kennedy in his 1961 inaugural address, had been vigorously pursued by him and his high-voltage, idealistic administration before he was assassinated after one thousand days in office.

It was still unknown how much of the Kennedy "magic kingdom of Camelot" aura would extend into the new and untested Johnson administration. It was as if a sophisticated, urbane Thomas Jefferson had handed the baton to a rustic, gauche Andrew Jackson.

In the eyes of much of the public at that time, the Johnson administration would not be able to hold a candle to that of Kennedy. The Kennedys, with their Boston accents and patina of sophistication, did not endear themselves to Johnson with his Texas drawl and "rough-as-a-corn-cob" manner when one of them labeled him Colonel Corn Pone.

Although we did not know it then, my family and I would live in Germany for the next four years. And before my career was over, I would cross the Atlantic a hundred times.

Rita and I were blessed with energy, enthusiasm, hope, ambition, confidence, and good health. We imagined we were cool and sophisticated, but our looks concealed our giddy excitement about moving to a distant country with a different culture and language. Nevertheless, we had no doubts about our ability to cope with the new lifestyle. We were beginning the adventure of our lives during the prime of our lives.

It was Rita's first trip to Germany. She had been in Europe earlier on a chaperoned college student tour, but Germany was off-limits due to postwar travel restrictions. It was my third business trip to Germany.

Even though the Third Reich, the scourge of Nazi Germany, was decisively blotted out by the unconditional victory of the Allied Forces nineteen years earlier, the raw scars—physical and psychological—throughout the country were still abundantly evident.

It seemed surreal that we were moving to a land that had such a hideous past and was so recently the archenemy of the US. She now seemed to be as docile as a contented cow chewing her cud in a pasture. Many older people who still had vivid memories of Germany's aggressive and barbaric behavior during two World Wars thought the image of a placid cow was a cunning illusion created by Germany to buy time to recuperate and prepare for her next bullying military adventure. But time would prove the skeptics need not have feared; most of the postwar German population was so appalled by the totality of her defeat—politically, socially, economically, and morally—that they were disposed toward pacifism.

Our Lufthansa pilots were well-scrubbed, confident, and competent—even a little cocky. The tall, multilingual stewardesses looked like models from Alpine skiing brochures. They were efficient and helpful.

Our children, five-year-old Kathy (Kathleen) and eighteen-month-old John, soon tired and slept on the floor in their pajamas in the open space reserved for an emergency exit. As was the custom of the times, Rita and I traveled in our best "going-to-church" clothes.

Although the age of international jet travel had been ushered in five years previously with the introduction of sleek, 150-passenger Boeing 707 jets, long-distance air travel still had a note of excitement and adventure. Our one-way air tickets each cost $350.

In the summer of 1963, six months before our move to Germany, my boss informed me that our employer—the John Deere company of Moline, Illinois—had decided to make a major capital investment to modernize its recently purchased tractor factory in Mannheim, Germany. The factory was part of the century-old German farm equipment firm, Heinrich Lanz AG. Lanz made tractors in Mannheim, grain-harvesting combines in Zweibrücken, Germany, and farm equipment for protected Spanish markets in Madrid.

When John Deere bought Lanz in 1956, its brand was well-known around the world—especially its best-known product, the Lanz Bulldog tractor. Bulldog was the common name for tractor in many parts of Germany. But the clunky Bulldog and many of the other Lanz products were obsolete, costly to manufacture, and unreliable. The Bulldog's principle market in the great wheat fields of East Germany was lost to the occupying communists. The transition from Lanz to John Deere ownership was still underway. The tractors and combines temporarily bore the name John Deere-Lanz. In a few years the company would drop the Lanz name.

In 1963, John Deere still had a long way to go to develop a viable business model suitable for its agricultural equipment business in Europe. It would be years until the markets were well-understood, the right management was in place, and the substantial financial losses were stemmed.

The Lanz factory and headquarters buildings in Mannheim were dug out of the rubble and patched together after repeated bombing by the US and its allies during World War II. Ninety percent of the industrial sections of the city were destroyed.

Some of Mannheim was still in ruins when John Deere bought the Lanz company. My brother, a GI, was stationed in Mannheim in the early 1950s. He said, "I could walk from the city center several miles to the railroad depot and see desolate, half-standing walls, and open cellars."

As a young engineer, I understood only a little of the overall company affairs; I only knew a narrow segment of the engineering and manufacturing side of the business. I could make a brick but I could not build a castle.

My boss told me a substantial corporate appropriation had been approved to modernize the Mannheim tractor factory. The appropriation included $8 million dollars ($50 million in 2014 dollars) to expand and rebuild its obsolete iron foundry located within the factory. The factory stood in the midst of a residential section of the city. Many environmental issues prevailed.

My boss said he was going to Germany to set up the groundwork for the foundry construction. He invited me to go with him on an introductory trip and then asked me to move my family to Germany to manage rebuilding the foundry—a multiyear project.

In my seven years of employment with John Deere, after discharge from the Army Chemical Center in Baltimore, I had worked mostly on engineering projects related to iron foundries. Iron castings from foundries were a fundamental component of farm tractors, diesel engines, and other farm equipment. Most John Deere factories included iron foundries.

Rita and I discussed moving to Germany: Would we be irreversibly pulling up our roots? How would it be for Rita to live outside the protective cocoon of her close family for the first time in her life? Why should we disrupt our comfortable, established life? Would we like living in a foreign country with a different culture? How would our small children fare?

Rita considered her life up to this time to be like a good stew made up of excellent ingredients but without enough spices to suit her tastes. Here was a chance for her to spice up the stew. As soon as we assured ourselves that the needs of our two small children could be met, she said, "Let's go." With her adventurous nature, impressive intelligence, puckish wit, unlimited energy, and natural social skills—she was usually the most noticed person in a room—she would likely fit into any culture.

I did not need to explain the nature of my work to Rita. Before I met her, and until we married, she and I worked in the same engineering office in John Deere's cramped, antiquated corporate headquarters. Rita worked as a secretary while waiting for a job to become available in her profession, teaching.

She was a pal to most of the 125 engineers, architects, and managers who worked in John Deere's engineering group—including the "gearheads," "nerds," and "wallflowers." She loved to banter with them all. The "socially challenged" and "eccentric" employees seemed to especially attract her attention; she savored the challenge of drawing them out of their shells and trying to rub some of her humor, good nature, and exuberance for life off onto them.

When we announced our marriage, one of the managers said to me, "I hear you're going to marry the 'Belle of the Engineering Department.'"

It will certainly be a duller place around here without her high-spirited presence." At that time, it was common for women to resign from their jobs when they married.

My managers never told me why they selected me to manage such a significant project in a distant place at such a young age. I guessed it was because I could work with minimum direction, I was reasonably ambitious, and I could maintain tight financial and schedule control of projects. It also helped that they knew Rita and had confidence in her ability to readily adjust to a new culture and to easily establish relationships with new people. I discounted another possibility: I may have been the only one who would accept the assignment.

I did not know then that I would not return to working as a design engineer. I would manage the engineering work of others for the rest of my career at John Deere and later after I started my own company. I eventually learned I had the ability to spot the strengths and flaws in the work of others even though I often could not do it myself.

I considered the new work assignment to be good for my professional career, but probably of equal importance, it seemed to be an adventure and an opportunity for expanding my family's personal life.

If I had been asked how my new assignment fit my professional goals, I would have said I did not have any concrete goals other than a vague desire to "do well and get ahead." This answer exhibited about as much forethought as the little boy who was asked, "What do you want to be when you grow up"? He answered, "I want to be an adult."

In regard to personal goals, it would be easier to explain: Rita and I were raised with a bedrock commitment to the values, traditions, and fundamental beliefs of our parents and close-knit families. We automatically adopted their values as our own.

Another personal goal—although less compelling—was for me to acquire financial security for myself and my family as soon as possible. I was driven in this direction because of memories from my youth during the Great Depression and the economic hardships in my rural South Dakota community. Accepting an overseas job meant a modest "hardship allowance" added to my salary. I planned to add this amount to my small, but slowly growing, savings and investment account. This goal was lower on Rita's agenda; she was raised in better economic circumstances than I.

My views on savings were reinforced by one of my salty and irreverent bosses who advised me to get my "go to hell money" together as soon as possible. Then he said I would never need to kowtow to him or anyone else; I could quit at any time and go elsewhere to work.

I had concern that Rita might not have enough to occupy her active mind in our new home. Without plenty to do she was like a caged tiger. A few years earlier she revved up her life by taking a part-time job as editor of a plumbing contractor trade journal. It involved face-to-face-communications and some travel—two of her favorite activities.

During the next several months we carefully planned to live for an indefinite time in Germany. We rented out our five-year-old colonial house for $175 per month and sold our two-year-old Ford for $500. The exhilaration during our six years of marriage and the birth of our two children had leveled off. We thought moving to another country and learning a new culture would juice up our lives.

I read books on German history and culture and took company-sponsored German language lessons. There was not enough time to do more than skim the surface. My German consisted mostly of learning two sentences: *Der Bleistift liegt auf dem Tisch* (The pencil lies on the table) and *Können Sie bitte mir sagen wo der Hauptbahnhof ist?* (Can you please tell me where the central railroad station is?).

Years later Rita confided, "I was depressed on my thirtieth birthday; I thought most of the excitement in my life was past. When the opportunity for moving to another country came up, I could see there was more excitement and adventure ahead for me."

During our flight over the Atlantic, we discussed the several noisy, boozy departure parties held for us by our friends and work colleagues and we spoke of the likely "downer" with Rita's mother, retired father, and sister due to our absence. They lived several blocks from our home in Rock Island, Illinois. We were an integral part of their lives with daily phone calls, frequent visits, and shared weekend meals.

It would be less difficult for me to be apart from my family. Although I was close to my mother—my father was deceased—and six siblings, we lived hundreds of miles apart as we pursued our lives, careers, and educations. One brother was a farmer; two were teaching or writing their PhD dissertations; one was an engineer; and the twins were members of Benedictine religious orders and both were teachers. We communicated mostly via letter writing and infrequent visits.

Rita and I were already somewhat familiar with the German culture and mentality because of our various associations with German-Americans. Two of Rita's grandparents came to America from Austria and northern France. Her father spoke German as a boy. Although my family culture was Irish, I was used to the industrious German farmers in our rural South Dakota community. Some could not pronounce "th" and "j" sounds; they called threshing machines "trashing machines" and jackets "yackets." Old ladies still prayed from prayer book pages dense with the forbidding German 𝔣𝔯𝔞𝔎𝔱𝔲𝔯 (Gothic) typeface. My mother recalled enough college German that she sent us to bed each night with a *"Gute Nacht."* The Hutterite farmers in our county still spoke a German dialect in their homes and religious services.

Rita prepared our children for the long flight by bringing John's favorite books, *Johnnie Tractor* and *Corny Corn Sheller*. She would re-read these "classics" to him hundreds of times during the next few years. Kathy maintained a firm connection to her past life by holding tightly onto Smokey, her large stuffed dog. Smokey already wore his second replacement plaid suit since my parents gave it to her shortly after her birth. Smokey would continue to occupy a position of prominence and honor on a chair in her bedroom for "all eternity."

During the flight, we read the *Chicago Tribune*—the world's greatest newspaper according to its bumptious owner, editor, and publisher, Colonel Robert McCormick. The entertainment section listed some of the popular American songs of 1963: "Blue Velvet" by Bobby Vinton; "Puff the Magic Dragon" by Peter, Paul, and Mary; and "The Days of Wine and Roses" by Henry Mancini. Sports journalists couldn't write enough about the 1963 Heisman Trophy winner, Roger Staubach.

On the editorial page, a perceptive journalist wrote that America's impressive record of military invincibility might not survive the controversial and expanding Vietnam War. His article started rolling down the hill a small snowball that would soon grow to a gigantic sphere and then, during the next few years, to an uncontrollable avalanche of frenzied protests against the questionable moral and political basis for US involvement in Vietnam. Many people, including me, did not think we should be in Vietnam at all, but we also thought we had to soldier on with our commitment while being conscious of our national and international prestige. At that time, the public had more confidence in the decisions of its elected Washington officials than it would in the future.

Every available scrap of news about the recent assassination of charismatic and glamorous John F. Kennedy and his large, hyperactive family saturated the front pages. Articles speculating on a conspiracy theory about his death were already starting to appear. Many could not believe that a puny worm like Lee Harvey Oswald could alone have extinguished the life of such a superior man as Kennedy.

Newly inaugurated President Johnson was developing programs of his own and attempting to step out of the mile-long shadow of the Kennedy administration. But it was a hard row for him to hoe; few remember the unfortunate president who succeeded towering Abraham Lincoln or the uninspiring prime minister who followed soaring Winston Churchill.

Our flight plan soon fell apart. The weather in Frankfurt was too stormy for landing, so our plane flew on to Cologne to refuel and wait out the storm. Eight hours later, we flew a hundred miles back to Frankfurt and arrived sleepless and bedraggled. A company driver had dutifully waited for us at the airport with his well-tended, company-owned Mercedes sedan.

Rita and I were still keyed up with excitement, so we stayed awake for the forty-five-mile autobahn drive to our new home in Heidelberg. The highway was bordered by snow-covered fields and sleeping evergreen forests. The ground under the trees looked like a Hansel and Gretel fairy story illustration with every fallen branch and twig raked up for utilization.

It was dusk when we arrived in Heidelberg. Although our household goods were already unpacked and set up in our rented house awaiting our occupancy, for the first night we stayed in a small, spic-and-span neighborhood hotel, Haus Fortuna. The German-speaking wife of a John Deere employee, who would later become Rita's best friend, knew our children would wake up in the middle of the night because of the eight-hour time change. She had wisely set in a supply of Rice Krispies and milk for a midnight snack.

During the six months prior to our move, I had worked in Germany to organize my work project. It was a busy time, but the event that I remember most vividly was sitting in a barbershop and being puzzled when my Italian barber simulated firing a pistol with his fist and index finger and excitedly said, "Boom, Boom. Kennedy ist tot." I thought it was odd behavior and had no idea what he was saying because of my inability at that time to speak German. When I returned to my hotel room an American colleague came to my room and quietly told me, "Kennedy has been assassinated."

The German people had great affection and respect for Kennedy, especially since his recent Berlin speech announcing unwavering support for West Germany as she faced the belligerent Russian bear to the east. He transfixed the German people when he said, "As a free man, I take pride in the words, *Ich Bin ein Berliner* (I am one of you)."

They were deeply disturbed when he was assassinated. A German journalist, steeped in ancient mythology, compared him to a golden god recalled from an ancient Greek myth; he had youth, beauty, courage, wisdom, grace, eloquence, and in the end tragedy. Kennedy's confidante, Daniel Patrick Moynihan, wrote, "To be Irish is to know that in the end the world will break your heart."

On my previous trip to Germany, I set up a home for my family. There was not a shortage of modern houses to rent at that time since the country was just nearing the finish of her postwar house and apartment building surge.

Rita and I favored traditional houses. I looked at many houses and apartments in Mannheim and the surrounding towns and villages, but found none interesting.

One weekend I drove around the neighborhoods of medieval Heidelberg, surrounded by steep mountains and bisected by the picturesque Neckar River. It was ten miles from Mannheim where I would be working. The Heidelberg suburb of Handschusheim—dating from Roman occupation times—was appealing. It was two kilometers from the center of Heidelberg.

I located and rented a traditional, unpretentious, but roomy, three-story row house in Handschusheim at Richard Wagner Strasse 11 on a narrow, quiet side street. The developer of the area was apparently a classical music buff; he named adjacent streets after Beethoven, Mozart, Haydn, and Bach. He must also have once vacationed in Italy for he had lettered "Villa Rosa" in the pediment over our front door. Our house owner was portly Herr Zabler. His name was visible on food packages in area grocery stores; his business was manufacturing noodles.

After I rented the house and organized it for our occupancy, I called Rita in Rock Island and said, "I think our life here will be good."

Unlike undamaged Heidelberg, Mannheim and adjacent Ludwigshafen—just across the Rhine River—were repeatedly pulverized and burned to rubble twenty years earlier during 150 allied bombing raids. They were logical targets because Mannheim was an industrial city and Ludwigshafen was the location of an enormous I.G. Farben chemical factory. With 37,000 employees before the bombing started, it manufactured "good and evil" products.

A colleague, who was a B-17 gunner, made bombing raids on the Ludwigshafen factory complex during the war. He said, "After the bombings, the only visible evidence of a factory remaining above ground was a shattered, meter-long pipe."

The Germans understood the logic of bombing strategic targets, but they were unforgiving for the massive allied firebombing of nonstrategic targets, such as Hamburg and Dresden, with a sickening loss of civilian lives. They conveniently disregarded the earlier indiscriminate German air raids and rocket attacks on residential sections of London and Coventry.

Hermann Göring, the morphine-addicted Reichsmarschall and commander and chief of the German air force, would be haunted for the rest of his life for having bragged early in the war, "No enemy bomber can reach the Ruhr (a major industrial center of Germany). If one ever should reach the Ruhr, my name is not Göring. You may call me Meyer (a common Jewish name)."

Heidelberg, a university town with a population of 140,000, was unscathed by bombs and war destruction. Some said it was off-limits for destruction so the US military forces would have a place to set up a garrison after the defeat of the Nazis. Indeed, five years after the war, it did become the headquarters for the US military forces in Europe.

Our household goods from Rock Island had been air-freighted to our newly rented house. As the new house renter, I had to repaint and re-wallpaper the high-ceilinged rooms; buy and install light fixtures; furnish wardrobes (rooms were built without closets); provide kitchen cabinets, counters, and appliances; buy heating oil for the five-hundred-gallon basement fuel tank; provide transformers to reduce voltage from 220 to 110 for our small appliances; and rewire our lamps to local codes. And I applied for telephone service and started the six-month waiting period for installation.

We checked out of Haus Fortuna the next morning and drove several blocks past fine old homes with neatly fenced yards to our rented house. From then on whenever we drove past our first-night hotel, Kathy would call it "The Tuna House."

Rita and our children saw our new home for the first time. The sight of familiar furnishings from our US house reassured them this really was going to be their new home. After they looked it all over and the children claimed their bedrooms, we sorted out the bedding and walked several blocks to a grocery store to buy food supplies.

I had set up Kathy's bedroom on the third floor, but she said it was "scary." We moved her down to a room beside our bedroom on the second floor that she would share for the next four years with John.

I was apprehensive about what Rita would think of my choices of paint and wallpaper for the house interior. My choices were pretty insipid, but she made no comment. I suspect she was so focused on what her new and different life would be like that she hardly noticed.

Our new 1963 red VW Beetle—license plate number HDV 232—was parked at the curb a few paces from our front door. I paid $1,400 for the "bug" with its sliding roof expecting it would be temporary until I could buy a larger car. I did not know then that it would adequately serve our needs for our entire four-year residency in Germany.

I found later that my car brand and model selection seemed odd to my German colleagues, who equated social and professional position to the kind of car driven. They expected me to drive a Mercedes, Volvo, Peugeot, Citroen, Opel Senator, or BMW.

Our "bug" was obviously manufactured on Monday morning—allegedly the time for low quality and "lemons." I had to remove and repair the defective engine more than once.

Sleep came easily the first night in our own beds in our new home after the previous day of time change and tension.

Our home would become a secure and happy bastion of transplanted America for us even though outside the door it was a different culture and country. It would quickly grow into a home-away-from-home; an inn; a coffee house; a forum for gossip, stories, and conviviality; a place for comforting and care giving; a center of excitement and friendship.

I rode to work in Mannheim with an American colleague the next day. It was a pleasant fifteen-minute drive, mostly on a limited-traffic autobahn. The autobahn was the same one driven by General George Patton several years earlier when his limousine was hit by a US Army truck, and he was mortally injured. I seldom drove past the collision spot that I did not think of the tragic accident.

The autobahn also passed a small airfield that was mostly used for amateur glider flying, a popular German sport. The airfield and adjacent autobahn recalled the 1930s when Hitler cheated on the World War I disarmament agreements that restricted military flying. He claimed the autobahns were for ground traffic but in reality the re-established Luftwaffe used them as landing strips for glider training and for testing new, advanced aircraft.

My return to work in my office in the Mannheim foundry was timely. There were major foundry equipment contracts ready to award. Companies were anxiously waiting to find out if they would be favored with orders based on their proposals—or "tenders" as they are called in British English.

And so began the next four years of working and living in Germany.

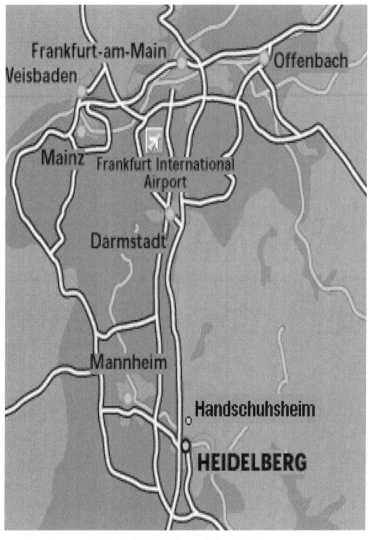

Map of Heidelberg, Mannheim, and Handschuhsheim Area

Company Name in Transition
Lanz to John Deere

President Kennedy in Dallas
Hours before His Assassination

CHAPTER 2

HEIDELBERG

I lost my heart in Heidelberg for all time,
On a balmy summer night.
As by the gates she said: "Good-bye my lover,"
That last sweet kiss, it did confirm once more,
I'd lost my heart in Heidelberg forever.
My heart still beats on Neckar's shore.
—Friedrich Vesely

HEIDELBERG

When filmmakers produce movies about the Middle Ages, they cannot find a better site for shooting than the Romantic city of Heidelberg with her population of 140,000. The city is located in the province of Baden-Württemberg in southwestern Germany. The south side of the province shares its border with Switzerland and France. It is set in a gorge cut by the Neckar River through the forested hills of the Odenwald, a low mountain range. Some of the houses are built into the steep valley walls with hairpin street curves that would challenge the twisting capability of a snake. The views are priceless.

Heidelberg is frequently chosen for movies, music fests, and operatic performances. One of the most famous productions is *The Student Prince,* an operetta later made into several movies. Who can forget the movie's stirring song, "Drink, Drink, Drink," sung by Mario Lanza in a *Bierstube* modeled after Heidelberg's two-century-old student haunt, *Zum Roten Ochsen* (Red Ox)? If patrons frequent the Red Ox long enough and are judged to be of good, all-around character, they may be honored with a personalized beer mug that will be reserved on a shelf behind the bar for their exclusive use.

The compact city of Heidelberg is endlessly walkable, and every view is a photo opportunity. The weather is mild enough to grow plants that are normally seen only in Mediterranean countries: almonds, figs, and an occasional olive tree. A poet portrayed Heidelberg as "The Pearl of the Neckar."

No visitor leaves the postcard city without a photo of the Old Bridge across the Neckar; the looming Heidelberg Castle located halfway up the *Königstuhl* (King's Throne), the steep hill overlooking the city; and the ancient city center.

The sandstone bridge, with its nine graceful arches, has stood for two hundred years except for a short time at the end of World War II when the retreating German Army blew up three of its arches. Goethe wrote, "This old bridge is more beautiful than all others in the world." The elaborate gate to the bridge from the old city side is incongruously guarded by bronze statues of apes.

A road rises from University Square in the city center up the steep mountainside to the hulking and dominating ruins, gardens, and partially rebuilt buildings of the landmark *Heidelberger Schloss* (Heidelberg Castle.)

The history of the castle site is as complex and varied as the family tree of an alley cat. The initial entry could be made 500,000 years ago. The bones of Heidelberg man, the probable forerunner of Neanderthal and modern man, were discovered near Heidelberg Castle in 1907. The next record of life on the castle site speaks of the presence of a Roman camp in 200 AD. Since Heidelberg Castle was built in 1200 AD, it has been burned, pillaged, blown up, abandoned, pulled down for salvage materials, expanded, patched up, and partially rebuilt.

For centuries it was the residence of kings, princes, dukes, margraves, regents, and counts as well as in-laws, down-at-the-heels relatives, and adventurers recuperating from military and political battles.

The castle, with its imposing towers, ramparts, and moat, continues to serve as a model for countless painters and photographers and as an inspiration for poets and writers.

For many years, the castle was the residence of the Palatine Elector, a prestigious position second only to a king or an emperor. The elector—one of seven—was entitled to vote for the election of the emperors of the Holy Roman Empire, a position that lasted for a thousand years starting with Charlemagne in 800 AD.

The brooding castle is a museum for diverse architectural styles: Gothic, Renaissance, Baroque, Roman, Greek, and a smattering of kitsch. A visit to the castle is like a fine, multicourse meal eaten slowly with worthwhile intervals between courses for the absorption of the tasty and sightly banquet.

Mark Twain lived, wrote, and honed his satirical wit for three months in a hotel near the Heidelberg Castle. He described the castle in his 1880 book, *Innocents Abroad:*

> A ruin must be rightly situated, to be effective. This one could not have been better placed. It stands upon a commanding elevation, it is buried in green woods, there is no level ground about it, but, on the contrary, there are wooded terraces upon terraces, and one looks down through shining leaves into profound chasms and abysses where twilight reigns and the sun cannot intrude. Nature knows how to garnish a ruin to get the best effect. One of these old towers is split down the middle, and one half has tumbled aside. It tumbled in such a way as to establish itself in a picturesque attitude. Then all it lacked was a fitting drapery, and nature has furnished that; she has robed the rugged mass in flowers and verdure, and made it a charm to the eye. The view half exposes its arched and cavernous rooms to you, like open, toothless mouths; there, too, the vines and flowers have done their work of grace. The rear portion of the tower has not been neglected, either, but is clothed with a clinging garment of polished ivy which hides the wounds and stains of time. Even the top is not left bare, but is crowned with a flourishing group of trees & shrubs. Misfortune has done for this old tower what it has done for the human character sometimes—improved it.

When we had out-of-town visitors in our home, we always took them to the castle on summer evenings for the *Schlossbeleuchtung* (Castle Illumination), an awesome fireworks and sound display to recall the destruction of the castle by the retreating French occupiers in 1689 and again in 1693.

A Heidelberg University curiosity is the *Studentenkarzer* (Student Prison) where, until World War I, boisterous students were locked up for intoxication, womanizing, and turning defecating pigs loose to soil the city streets. The prison walls and ceiling were used as slates for songs, verses (some written in Latin and Greek), stories, artwork, and graffiti. Student prisoners were temporarily "paroled" from the prison to attend classes.

In the past, Heidelberg University students dueled according to a set of rigid rules and traditions. One of the objectives was to acquire facial scars that would be regarded as marks of honor. Some rubbed the raw wounds with salt to make them look more daunting. Otto von Bismarck, creator of the modern German nation in the nineteenth century, attended the university. He said, "The scars are proof of courage." Dueling was especially common with elite Austrian and Prussian students. Husband-seeking women looked for the scars to help identify educated men with wealth and prestige. Men with dueling scars turned their scar side to photographers and portrait artists to show their "badges of courage" in the best light.

I have a prominent facial scar from a childhood farm accident. When I first took German lessons, my forthright tutor asked how I acquired it. When I said it was from being trampled by a cow, she exclaimed, *"Eine Kuh. Nicht möglich!"* (A cow! Impossible!).

The swift Neckar River is a pleasant Heidelberg focal point with its armada of bad-tempered white swans, paddleboats for children, and cargo boats on their way between the river's origin in the Black Forest and the Rhine River in nearby Mannheim. A cargo boat usually had a living cabin, with potted geraniums in the windows, where the boatman's family sometimes lived. Some had short cranes on the stern to off-load the family's minicar for a spin around ports of call.

We often took our children for Sunday rides on the paddleboats anchored along the grassy riverbanks, but first we had to settle jurisdictional and navigational disputes with the confrontational white swans. A poke with a paddle or pole simply increased their ire and determination to protect their rightful territorial waters. The swans maintained a tight segregation policy by rigidly confining the resident Siberian swan geese to their territorial waters a short distance upstream.

While Mark Twain boated on the Neckar in 1867, his three-year-long writer's block ended. An idea about rafting came to him that enabled him to complete his stalled writing of *The Adventures of Huckleberry Finn*, one of his best-known novels.

On the opposite side of the river from the castle is the start of a steep, two-hundred-step path up the mountainside to *Philosophenweg* (Philosophers Way) where a flight of African, rose-winged parakeets can sometimes be spotted. The stepped path, called *Schlangenweg* (Snake Way), twists past tiny, well-tended gardens and vineyards at each landing—

some with gardening sheds or pergolas. Lookout spots provide dramatic overviews of the city.

Professors and students from Heidelberg University have trudged the gnarly way for centuries to contemplate the mysteries of life, craft lofty intellectual works, and plot their futures. The awesome overlook to the river, city, and castle is one of the best in all of Europe.

When we hiked on Philosophers Way on Sunday afternoons, it was for less elevating purposes; it provided exercise for our dog, gave us good supper appetites, and improved our sleeping.

Heidelberg and the US military forces were firmly bonded together by the 1960s. In early 1945, General George Patton's 3rd Army sprinted across France and into Germany after the Normandy invasion. It was the beginning of the defeat of the Nazi Army.

Patton impressed the German General Staff and High Command and others with his dashing and brilliant military victories. The Sultan of Morocco said of him after his earlier North African successes, "The lions in their den tremble when he approaches." Some exhausted, battle-weary GIs thought otherwise because of his grinding, relentless pressure for lightning speed, showmanship, aggression, and quest for glory. Awed senior German generals regarded Patton as a "classical warrior with mythical stature."

Patton's commander for capturing Heidelberg and the surrounding area was German-speaking Brigadier General William Beiderlinden, who knew the local history, language, and culture. Beiderlinden met with six courageous and daring, but unauthorized, Heidelberg municipal officials outside the city and negotiated its surrender. He gave the authorities two choices: surrender or see the summary destruction of their town. They accepted the surrender option and agreed to take it to the military authorities in the city for their approval.

The authorities made a harrowing return trip across the Neckar River and back into the city. Had they been captured by the Nazis, they would have been summarily executed for treason. They successfully persuaded the remaining *Wehrmacht* officers that it was futile to resist and they should surrender. If they agreed, Beiderlinden's seasoned troops, tanks, and guns would peacefully enter the city the next day at dawn. They agreed and the next morning on March 30, 1945 the American Army crossed the Neckar and peacefully occupied Heidelberg.

The streets and squares were silent and empty, but behind the window curtains, countless, wary eyes watched as they tried to imagine their fate. Many were grateful that their nightmare was ending and that their captors were not Russians; the words "Russia," "murder," "rape," and "looting" were often spoken in the same sentence.

The bell in the Church of the Holy Spirit, overlooking the town, tolled in the dawn on the day of the occupation as it had for the last five centuries oblivious to the drama below. It had all happened before, and the bell would continue tolling on into future centuries in its dignified and nonjudgmental fashion.

Patton would likely have handled the negotiation with the Heidelberg authorities more harshly than Beiderlinden. While interrogating a captured German general in English at another location he said, "I speak German very well but I will not demean myself to do so now." He then berated the general for being taken in by the evil Nazis.

Patton persistently talked to his staff and troops of his desire to kill as many Germans as possible. He once stood on the back of a half-track and gave this unambiguous and salty advice to a tank unit ready to go into battle: "Go up there and kill those Kraut SOBs!"

When the war ended, General Patton established his personal residence in Heidelberg. On the day before he was to fly home to plan for his retirement, he and his chief of staff, Major General Hobart Gay, set out in his black 1938 Cadillac limousine for nearby Mannheim to hunt pheasants and sightsee. A US Army truck collided with the limousine. The accident, although relatively minor, mortally injured Patton. As he lay on his deathbed in a Heidelberg military hospital, his wife Bea, his lifelong confidante, flew to Germany to be at his side.

Patton had a deep knowledge of Greek and Roman history, myths, and legends. It is easy to imagine him thinking of his life as a classical Greek tragedy performed in an ancient Athens theater, with the final curtain of the last act about to be drawn. His last request was that the GI truck driver who drove into his car not be prosecuted.

Patton's Heidelberg residence looked like a stately old hunting lodge. It had been summarily commandeered for his use by the US Army as was frequently done when US troops first occupied Germany. Rita and I attended a dinner in the attractive lodge after Patton died and it was returned to its rightful owner. Rita and the lodge owner's wife were both members of the German-American Women's Club, a group organized to help salve old animosities.

The economy of Heidelberg was primarily based on the university, tourism, publishing, and printing press manufacturing. Because none had strategic value to the war, the city was not a bombing target.

The venerable and highly respected Heidelberg University, with its thirty thousand students, was seven hundred years old. It recalled the ancient learning academies from more than two thousand years earlier in Athens. The accomplishments of its multidisciplined teachers and graduates were world-renowned.

But the university also had a far darker side. Early in the war, Hitler converted the university into a forum for his savage Nazi ideology. The Nazis sacked all Jews from the faculty and student body. Most of them—as well as the other Jewish city residents—were taken to their grim fate in the Dachau Concentration Camp. The two Heidelberg synagogues were torched. The Nazis also did a lot of other burning throughout the country: the Reichstag (federal parliament building), bonfires to commemorate Hitler's birthday, censored books and literature, and inmates of concentration camps. When the war ended, Heidelberg University quickly returned to normal after purification by a rigorous denazification process.

Another stain on Heidelberg's character was Albert Speer, Hitler's architect—Hitler was intensely interested in architecture and art—and Minister of Armaments and War Production. His prosperous family made its home in Heidelberg. Speer employed hundreds of thousands of forced laborers—Jews, Slavs, and others—in factories where they were mercilessly and systematically starved and worked to death. If the prisoners were ill, late for work, weak, violators of factory work rules, exhausted, unable to meet work norms, or disobedient, they were summarily exterminated. After the Nuremberg trials, Speer was sentenced to twenty years in Spandau Prison in Berlin. In 1981 he died and was buried in Heidelberg.

Heidelberg had an unfortunate and tragic problem to deal with in the 1960s and for many years thereafter. A German pharmaceutical company developed a "miracle drug," thalidomide. It was intended to cure colds, reduce pain, and eliminate morning sickness for pregnant women. Nine months after its introduction, more than 10,000 babies were born with appalling birth defects—flippers for hands, deformed legs, and missing limbs. Heidelberg became a treatment and rehabilitation center for many of the afflicted victims.

It was not unusual to see thalidomide victims publicly as they grew up and tried to lead normal lives. While eating in a Heidelberg restaurant, I saw a young armless man sitting alone as he ordered his meal. A stranger, without self-consciousness, kindly and graciously cut his food and placed it in his mouth. In Germany, it is common to share restaurant tables with strangers when there are no open tables.

John Deere's senior European executive leased the Springer mansion high up a mountainside overlooking the Neckar River, the Old City, and Heidelberg Castle. The Springer Publishing Company had been a major publishing presence in Germany for many decades.

Arriving as a guest at the Springer house was like approaching a spook house. A small trolley ran on steep narrow-gauge railroad tracks to take guests hundreds of feet from the street level up the mountainside to the house. In the dusk, riders with good imaginations could envision scary creatures—wolves, bears, and witches from the pages of Grimm's Fairy Tales—lurking behind the gnarled oaks, craggy rocks, and dense bushes. The car was pulled by an electric winch and cable. The view over the valley from the house at sunset was spectacular enough to make even the soaring eagles "ooh and aah."

The enchanting Romantic City of Heidelberg is like no other. It's a fine place for lovers to kiss, dreamers to fantasize, and philosophers to ponder. Theologians can seek divine guidance and geniuses can theorize on the origin of the universe. It's a haven for artists to daub, musicians to perform, and photographers to click. It's a refuge where poets can rhyme, writers can pen, and students can cram and carry on with carefree abandon before assuming the burdens of adulthood. It's a location where tourists can gawk, boaters can row, and hikers can ramble. It's never more than a short stroll to a restaurant or bar where diners can tuck it away and drinkers can quaff. And it's a safe and undisturbed retreat where loafers can pass the time of day and old people can dream of times past while dozing on park benches surrounded by rose bushes.

Heidelberg

Heidelberg Castle

Old Heidelberg Bridge

Garden Along Philosopher's Way

Paddle Boat on Neckar River
John, Frank, and Kathy

Swans on the Neckar River

HEIDELBERG

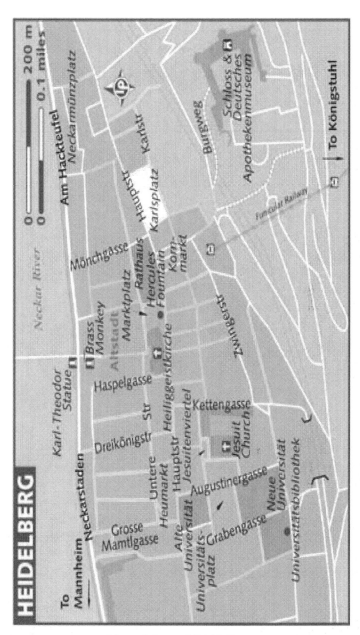

Map of Central Heidelberg

CHAPTER 3

OVERSEAS EXPANSION

With 85% of the world's cultivated land outside the US, overseas expansion for John Deere is a no-brainer.

European Hay Wagons—1940s

When I first worked as an engineer for the John Deere company in 1955, it was a medium-sized midwest business with annual sales—primarily farm equipment—of $300 million. The company president, who was John Deere's greatgrandson, had just died. His urbane 40-year-old son-in-law, William Hewitt from John Deere's San Francisco sales branch, was elected to succeed him.

Hewitt, who looked as if he was sent from a Hollywood central casting office as the leading man for a movie, set an aggressive new course for the company. He put dynamic, broad-thinking people in key positions, shifted the company image to a more cosmopolitan basis, set demanding objectives, and targeted growth. One of the driving forces during the quarter century of Hewitt's leadership was aggressive overseas expansion.

He knew the company had achieved impressive success since its founding in 1837 based on John Deere's invention of the steel plow, but he thought it had become too cautious and ingrained to meet the ambitious changes and growth objectives that he envisioned.

Hewitt soon took "tree-shaking" action. One of his many interests was the design and appearance of new products, factories, and offices. He insisted that they be designed by imaginative engineers, stylists, and architects.

At the suggestion of Robert McNamara, his Harvard Business School classmate and the president of Ford Motor Company, Hewitt engaged Eero Saarinen, a world-renowned, Finnish-American architect, to design John Deere's imaginative new seven-story corporate headquarters on a rustic 1,400-acre site overlooking the rich bottomland of the Rock River Valley in Moline, Illinois. The new office, completed in 1964, reflected the character of John Deere's agricultural business: earthy, exposed steel (cor-ten) structure; surrounding fields of corn and soybeans and old farm buildings; reflecting lake with geese and swans, reminiscent of a farm pond; and a showroom for displaying equipment against a backdrop of artifacts from rural America. The company headquarters soon became a tourist attraction and a model for many other new corporate campuses.

The new building projected the image Hewitt wanted for the prestigious international company that he envisioned John Deere would soon become. Paul Goldberger, the architecture critic for the *New York Times*, described the building and site: "one of the most beautifully sited structures in contemporary American architecture, with an atmosphere of utter dignity and serenity."

Simultaneously in St. Louis, the majestic Gateway Arch—also designed by Saarinen—was built. The arch and the John Deere headquarters were both grounded on symbolism of the land and the west: nature (rainbow and earth); vast prairies; rivers—Rock, Missouri, and Mississippi; and people associated with the west—Jefferson, Lewis & Clark, and Deere as well as hunters, trappers, farmers, ranchers, explorers, miners, blacksmiths, missionarys, merchants, and builders.

Hewitt insisted that John Deere products have the fingerprints of industrial designer Henry Dreyfus on the blueprints. Dreyfus was renowned for his design of many other products: typewriters, telephones, locomotives, pens, and vacuum cleaners.

When Hewitt came to Moline, the John Deere Board of Directors was made up of older company officials; some were John Deere descendants. He brought new directors to the board and he joined other business and academic boards to help him discover and bring home new ideas.

Hewitt broadened the perspective of John Deere management with continuing education programs; exposure to other cultures and business models; selectively hiring mid-career people with proven specialty skills;

involvement in Asian affairs; and engagement of well-known artists and speakers to perform at all levels throughout the company.

He set his eye on John Deere becoming the industry leader for farm equipment. At that time International Harvester—based on the invention of the mechanical grain reaper and founded six years earlier than John Deere—held the lead. Hewitt said, "We are not aiming to be a runner-up. We are aiming to be first in all our business activities." Ultimately John Deere would be first by a long shot, but there would be many intervening miles of good and bad road to travel first.

Other strong competitors were Minneapolis-Moline, Allis Chalmers, J.I. Case, Massey Ferguson, Claas, Deutz, and Ford. Many of them—including giant International Harvester—would eventually go under or drastically restructure their operations because of the prolonged economic downturn in the 1980s. Claas and Deutz (German companies), however, survived. I was familiar with most of these companies and their farm equipment from my boyhood days growing up on a South Dakota farm.

After establishing manufacturing operations in Mexico and Argentina, John Deere bought Heinrich Lanz AG, an ailing German farm equipment company, in 1956. Other overseas companies in France, South Africa, England, and elsewhere were also acquired.

Satisfying the unique farm equipment buying needs and habits of customers in dozens of countries in Europe, the Middle East, and Africa was a marketing and engineering challenge. The Dutch needed a slow tractor "creeper" speed for planting tulips. The Germans and others required power takeoffs (shafts to operate equipment) on the fronts of their tractors. The French needed yellow head lights to satisfy their road laws. Iraqi customers needed wagons to catch their combine harvesters' straw, which they used as a binder for making adobe building bricks. The challenges were not always met with empathy and dispatch; sometimes American and overseas business processes and practices clashed.

John Deere engineering and marketing departments in Europe were managed by a combination of US and European employees. It took time to build trust, understanding, teamwork, and cultural appreciation among them.

For example, a different way of advertising and product promotion was needed in Germany. Major new product introduction shows in America included hullabaloo (country music and entertainment) as standard fare. Germans viewed this as frivolous; what counted for them was serious technical information on horsepower, efficiency, and revolutions per minute. Music and entertainment were for after-work hours.

Some US employees could find it perilous for their careers to accept overseas assignments. They were separated from their mentors and out of sight for career advancements. When they were later repatriated to the US, their overseas work was sometimes not well understood or appreciated. Some left the company. But for others, overseas work was recognized and the experience leveraged them to higher positions. The European sales director who sat in an office across the hall from my work cubicle in the company's regional Heidelberg office later became the John Deere CEO. And another young American, also working in European sales, rose rapidly and eventually became CEO.

It was hard for employees to stop calling the overseas business "foreign" as if it were an alien thing or a speck in the eye. The terms "global" and "worldwide" slowly became the accepted words to describe the company's expanding international business.

The language of international companies is English. Overseas managers and professionals had to learn English if they had any hope of career advancements. Most Americans who were transferred overseas were less diligent in learning the local languages.

Jokes abounded about the use of English and the alleged domineering nature of American management; a German friend facetiously said when his colleagues were not responsive enough to his orders in German, he switched to English to get prompt action.

I visited an Opel auto factory (General Motors subsidiary) in Kaiserslautern, Germany. An employee joked that the day before, company visitors from Detroit came to the factory. When they stepped outside for lunch, the visitors put up their umbrellas even though it was a sunny day. They explained, "But it's raining in Detroit."

Several of us worked fairly diligently to learn German with various degrees of success. I explained to a friend, "I can speak fluent bad German if it is spoken slowly with the vocabulary of a ten-year-old, and the subject is engineering and manufacturing."

In the mid-1960s, worried teams of John Deere executives and employees met in European hotels and conference rooms in communities where the company owned businesses. They were trying to improve sales and speed up achieving profitability. Some of the local managers complained that they had to spend so much time preparing for executive visits, they had little time to manage their factories and sales offices. Times were difficult; it seemed to some—even a few in senior management positions—that success in the European markets was a mirage.

Selling equipment in competition with many smaller, locally entrenched companies was difficult. Farmers were loyal to their traditional tractor and combine suppliers. John Deere's hope that the competitors would quickly fade away in the face of a more powerful company with better products was wishful thinking.

It was a difficult time for the senior John Deere executives. They had to explain to the board of directors why overseas sales and profit objectives were not being met.

Some senior officers and board members became impatient with the large and persistent European losses. They advocated a quick way out by forming a new company combining John Deere's overseas operations with the assets of another international equipment company. This option was never acted upon.

The John Deere factories in Germany have highly visible, cone-shaped water towers that look like giant martini glasses. The German financial press derisively called them "dollar funnels."

During my time in Germany, a black cloud persistently hung over the company's European business; the financial and marketing problems were like a chronic headache.

The modernization of the factories and products, however, moved along at a steady pace. As management and technical problems were sorted out, the factories were eventually able to supply the required equipment to the market.

My limited role while I lived in Germany was to work as an engineer and assist in providing modern manufacturing facilities. But due to the close-knit nature of John Deere's American resident community, I had the opportunity to associate with people in all areas of the business, especially marketing and sales. By listening and asking questions, I had the chance to hear something about most aspects of the company's European business. Until years later, after I gained more experience and after I started my own business, I did not fully appreciate that the marketing and financial needs of businesses are among the most intractable and difficult areas to manage.

After years of heartbreaks and losses, the expansion by John Deere into overseas markets—especially in Europe—would prove to be an immense success. The experiences gained during the early difficult years would become the building blocks for further worldwide company growth. Eventually, overseas sales would approach half of the company's total sales. History would define William Hewitt and his management team as international business visionaries.

Some of John Deere's Competitors

Early John Deere Logo

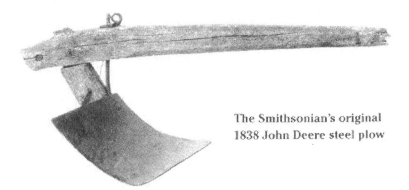

The Smithsonian's original 1838 John Deere steel plow

First John Deere Steel Plow

CHAPTER 4

LIVING IN GERMANY

*If you reject the food, ignore the customs, fear the religion,
and avoid the people, you might better stay home.*
—James Michener

Villa Rosa (Lyons Home)
Richard Wagner Strasse 11, Handschsheim

If I had hired an architect to design a house in Heidelberg, I would have modeled it after our rented row house at Richard Wagner Strasse 11 where I lived with my family for four years in the mid-1960s. On the ground floor were a living room, dining room, kitchen, and half bath. Each of the upper two floors had three bedrooms and a full bath. The house was built over a full basement exposed to the back yard and under a semi-finished attic. The floors throughout were configured in an oak herringbone design. The sturdy, curved ground-floor-to-attic stairs and ample wood trim demonstrated the skillfulness of the builder.

Floor designations in Germany and throughout Europe confuse Americans. The first floors are ground floors. The next floor up is the first floor.

The tan stucco exterior of our house and red tile roof were set off by a pair of magnolia trees in the small, fenced front yard. The back of the house, with iron balconies off each room, supported mature wisteria vines with ropey trunks that extended to the roof. The vines profusely bloomed twice a year with lush clusters of lavender flowers. The fenced backyard was large enough for a flower garden, a small lawn, and our children's sandbox and play equipment.

A visitor who had been a soldier in the US Army during the war said when his unit lobbed low-intensity explosives into houses like ours to dislodge soldiers, the loosely set roof tiles lifted off like dry, autumn leaves flying around in a puff of wind. The undamaged tiles could be reset and the houses quickly re-inhabited.

Our house was well-heated with hot water radiators. We reordered heating oil annually and pumped it into a steel tank in the basement.

There was no garage—and limited need for one. The weather was mild and a parking place at the curb was understood to be reserved for the use of the adjacent house occupant.

When we vacated the house four years later, we decided if we ever returned to live, we would try to rent the same house again.

Moving from the US to Germany and its different culture was relatively easy for us. John Deere already had a number of US families living in the Mannheim area and the US military was a huge presence throughout all of West Germany. Other large international companies were also present. The resident John Deere employees provided a safety net for newcomers. With their help, Rita and I rapidly settled into the local domestic and social routine.

West Germany was still heavily occupied by US military forces. Streets, restaurants, bars, stores, historical sites, ski-slopes, trains, and airports teemed with GIs and their families, civil service personnel, and military contractors.

US military personnel were especially prevalent in Bavaria where many of the fine holiday resorts had been requisitioned at the end of the war. GIs enjoyed many privileges: special car licenses, tax-free gasoline, well-stocked military commissaries, schools, and medical facilities.

Some GIs chose to live exclusively within their military compounds. Others "went native." They learned to speak German and associated mostly with German people. There were many intercultural marriages.

Rita soon learned to drive our VW bug although for the first few weeks, it was a "herky-jerky" business; she had never before handled a stick-shift. She had the full-time use of our car because I rode to work in Mannheim with a fellow employee who drove a company car.

With Rita's long list of friends to visit, Kathy's school affairs, scout activities, bridge games, coffee gatherings, clubs, and local tours for visitors, the car engine seldom cooled down. Heidelberg and the surrounding area soon became her "hometown" and most people whom she met quickly became her friends.

She could easily walk to neighborhood stores for groceries, drugs, meat, bread, and dairy products. All shoppers carried their purchases in their own reusable mesh bags. The waste of throw-away bags would be unacceptable to the thrifty Germans, who still vividly remembered acute postwar shortages. Small merchants traditionally catered to the tastes, needs, and interests of their clients with the utmost helpfulness, courtesy, and kindness.

The first time Rita went to the nearby grocery store, she asked for daily milk delivery service to our house. The proprietor was not willing to deliver when she found that we lived so close to the store. Daily food shopping was the norm; refrigerators, the size of large beer coolers, were only intended to hold a day's supply of food.

All shopping had to be carefully scheduled; on Sundays, stores and gas stations closed. A few designated drug stores remained open for emergencies.

We enrolled our daughter, Kathy, in nearby Mark Twain Village Elementary School. This facility was previously a part of a German military compound. The school was operated by the US Department of Defense. It was like a transplanted piece of America with all the trimmings: US style study courses, bus service to our doorstep, sports, Girl Scouts, American teachers, and US-style, extracurricular activities. The military accepted nonmilitary American students for a cash tuition payment.

Rita was educated in all-girls convent schools. Many of her US schoolmates and friends were from "white glove" social circles. She was not accustomed to the soldier's use of earthy English. Kathy's army bus sometimes had barracks graffiti written on its side. Rita asked a friend what some of the words meant. Her friend explained the words but was astonished that a thirty-four-year-old married woman had led such a protected life.

Our social life was usually with other American or British people, although we also socialized with Germans when there was an adequate combination of English and German speaking skills. We had an active social life with a wide variety of people. Much of it was due to Rita's popularity and personality. People were attracted to her as if she were magnetic; most of them wanted her to become their friend.

She was easily identifiable by her signature clothes: Chanel style suits for day wear and swishy, pleated cocktail dresses for evenings.

My favorite of all of her coats was her Kinsale cloak that we bought for a pittance in the village of Kinsale in southern Ireland. It was a floor-length, flowing, black wool robe with a wide hood and exposed Kelly green silk lining. She wore it for years on St. Patrick's Day, when she looked like the inspiration for the ancient Irish ballad about the loveliest lass in the county:

Star of the County Down

From Bantry Bay up to Derry Quay
From Galway to Dublin Town
No maid I've seen like the fair colleen
That I met in the County Down

Inviting friends to our home for an evening of high-spirited conversation and a wine-fortified dinner was often our way of socializing. Few were the company visitors to Germany who did not eat a meal in our dining room. I came home from work one evening and found our dinner guest was already in our living room with Kathy. He said Rita was at the hospital emergency room with three-year-old John. In John's usual fashion, he had ignored Rita's sound advice not to run with a scissors in his hand. He fell down a flight of outside concrete stairs and stuck the blades in his forehead; the damage was quickly repaired with a few stitches. Rita was terrified that he had put out an eye. For years, Kathy reminded all who would listen that John was the "naughty baby" and she was the "good baby."

A heavyset, middle-aged German woman rang our doorbell a few weeks after we established our Heidelberg residency. She said, "Me Frau Wörle. Me clean house. Me work hard. OK?" Rita quickly replied, "OK."

Frau Wörle stayed with us for four years. She kept our house spotless and occasionally cooked my supper when Rita and the children were away. Her homemade spätzle (noodles) were a welcome treat. She soon became a warm and welcome part of our household. We never knew who sent her to our door to ask for work.

She loved two-year-old John. She called him *Schatzi* (little treasure.) When Rita, Kathy, and I were away on trips, she and her husband sometimes took John to stay with them in their apartment and to go away for weekend bus trips to the mountains and forests along with their tent and camping equipment. When we returned, John did not always like to come home because of the fun and freedom he had while on outings with the Wörles.

On weekends Rita and I tried to sleep late. Kathy liked to get up early and wake us to prepare her breakfast. She knew we would be cross with her for waking us too early so she poked John to make him cry until we got up to care for him. Decades later she admitted to her "treachery."

Many of the resident US military personnel in the Heidelberg area lived in rented housing throughout the community. They called it "living on the economy." Army Captain Calderwell and his wife lived next door to us. He drove a Jaguar sport car. When he came to our house for social visits, he lowered his six foot plus frame onto our living room floor and pretended he was driving his "Jag." He noisily shifted, revved up the engine, honked, backfired, and skidded his tires—all verbally. My children loved his playful, raucous visits.

For hours each day, our next door neighbor lady and her dog stared out the open casement window with their arms—front legs in the case of the dog—resting on a small oriental rug hung out over the windowsill; houses did not have window screens. The pair took in the fresh air and maintained vigil over all neighborhood activities.

It was common to hang carpets, bedding, and clothing out windows to air them in the sun and fresh air. Germans considered as much fresh air and sun as possible to be healthy, hygienic, and wholesome.

A neighbor rented out her third-floor rooms to university students. Thin ropes sloped down from the dormer windows to the front yard picket fence with an attached tin can fashioned for efficiently sending notes or small items up and down. It saved walking up the stairs.

When rooms were rented out, it was easy to maintain privacy for the house occupants because of the German habit of closing all doors when entering or leaving rooms.

Our neighborhood was quiet and safe. There was a small, restful municipal rose garden with benches a few doors away from our house.

Kathy liked to ride her bicycle through the garden and around the community to look over the fences at the flower gardens and occasionally at caged or leashed pets. When John was a little older, she raced around with him on their bright red, foot-powered rollers (scooters), the universal transportation vehicle for local children.

Spring in Germany was like a trip to fairyland with fruit trees—apples, pears, plums, and cherries—blossoming like billowing white and pink clouds. Thrifty landowners enjoyed the trees' beauty in the spring and bountiful harvest in the fall. Thriftiness was also evident in the countryside and small villages. Very small plots of land were often planted into tiny vineyards or hayfields.

On our frequent weekend drives, we often drove through the lush farmland surrounding Heidelberg and Mannheim. Most of the farm crops were similar to those grown in the US Midwest—oats, rye, wheat, and barley—but we never saw corn fields. Orchards and turnip fields were also prevalent. The giant turnips were fed to farm animals. We occasionally saw plots of hops with their pyramid-shaped drying oasts (hops-drying kilns) and extensive vineyards, often on steep hills facing south to catch the sun rays.

Farm layouts were different from what we knew in the US; the fields were smaller and the houses and farm buildings were clustered in villages rather than on each farm.

Wildlife was valued and conserved in Germany, but after millennia of human development, the animal species and habitats had greatly evolved from earlier eras. Some of the remaining animals were deer, badgers, foxes, hedgehogs, hares, owls, wild boar, and adders.

There were also majestic storks, recently brought back from near extinction. Chimneys of large houses and church steeples were sometimes surrounded near the top with iron work suitable for stork nests that could reach two meters in width. To have white storks, with their black-tipped wings and tails, in residence on the roof was considered a special treat.

Because of the favorable and stable exchange rate between the German Deutschmark and the US dollar (one Deutschmark exchangeable for one US quarter), frequent weekend family excursions were affordable. Rita and I favored places of historical and picturesque interest for our weekend outings. It took other criteria to satisfy and entertain Kathy and John. For weeks after we spent a weekend in the quaint and historical village of Colmar in Alsace, France, the children could only talk of Figaro, the resident, striped gray cat.

When Rita's parents and sister lived with us for several summers, her father often sat in the small neighborhood rose garden and talked to other strollers, visitors, and dogs. He remembered a little of the German that he had learned in school as a child in Rock Island, Illinois, and from his mother, who as a teenager had emigrated to the US from Alsace in northeast France.

My mother and four other family members also visited us for several weeks as they recharged their batteries in the middle of a lengthy European tour.

Rita reveled in the comradeship of our visitors and houseguests and the opportunity to share with them the adventure of living in a different culture and the endless sights of our Heidelberg community. She liked to rent a Volkswagen minibus to drive our visitors to places of interest—often on overnight trips. She fit in well with aggressive German drivers with her heavy accelerator foot.

I welcomed visits from Rita's father. He bought and read the same kind of books that I liked, and he gave them to me when he was through with them. His running verbal book reviews were standard dinner table entertainment whether other diners were interested or not. He liked to read history and biography books as well as books about architecture and adventure.

My father-in-law, a fellow engineer, never gave me professional advice, but he had many adages that I found useful: End meetings five minutes before they're over. When you direct a person to do a task, never tell him how to do it. People who wait for green lights get left behind.

While I was away on a business trip, he took the family to supper at the nearby Tannhäuser Hotel dining room; most European hotels include good restaurants. While eating, John had a major rupture in his diapers. To contain the mess, my father-in-law pulled off the tablecloth and, with the help of the waiter, completely wrapped him in it to take him home for cleanup. The waiter received what was probably the biggest tip of his life.

When John was two and a half years old and "house broken," Rita enrolled him in St. Vitus School as a pre-kindergarten student; he attended the school for three-years. It was less than two blocks from our house on a quiet street seldom visited by town residents or tourists.

The school was connected to the oldest church in the area, originally built in 1050. The church crypts contained the elaborate stone tombs of knights and noble personages from the dim past. Full size stone carvings of the tomb occupants stretched out on top of the tombs. The men were resplendent in armor and mail, while eternally gripping their weapons.

The ridiculously exaggerated mounding of the lower armor sections attested to the knights' pride in their masculinity.

We occasionally attended Sunday church services in the St. Vitus church, but more often we drove several miles to Mark Twain village to the US military chapel so we could hear mass in English.

John dressed like all of the other boys in his school—lederhosen and a green felt hat with a leather shoulderbag containing a fresh roll for his midmorning snack. Rita walked with him to and from school. His nurturing teacher was Tante (Aunt) Heidi. John learned to speak fluent German. He made friends easily with his schoolmates and developed an easygoing, self-confident—and sometimes rambunctious—style that stayed with him for life.

John soon learned a children's nursery rhyme from Tante Heidi and taught it to Rita. They recited it endlessly:

Alle Meine Entchen

Alle meine Entchen
Schwimmen auf dem See
Köpfchen in das Wasser
Schwänzchen in die Höh.

All My Little Ducks

All my little ducks
Swimming on a lake
Little heads in the water
Little tails in the air.

St. Martins Day on 11 November is an ancient agricultural and religious holiday in much of Europe. To start the celebration, a man representing St. Martin rides a horse through the village streets leading a goose with a string around its neck and a parade of children carrying illuminated paper lanterns with carefully placed candles inside. The children sing special songs honoring the occasion. John's kindergarten participated in the parades.

While on home leave to the U.S just after a St. Martin's Day celebration, John looked out the plane window as we landed in Chicago in the evening and saw the orderly, brightly lit car traffic on the streets below. He said, "Oh, Mutti (mommy) look at the *Laterne Parade* down there."

She said, "No, John, those are the headlights of cars driving on the streets."

He seemed to accept her explanation, but several days later he said to his grandfather, "You should have seen the great *Laterne Parade* we saw from our plane window." There was no uncertainty in his mind about what he had seen!

Another place where we attended church was Stift Neuberg, an ancient Benedictine monastery on a bluff overlooking the Neckar River Valley and the villages below. The church had individual, carved oak seats facing the sides of the altar for each of the monks. It was surrounded by orchards, fields, a school, and a dairy farm. Sunday donations were "extracted" by a bearded, grizzled, elderly monk who looked like a gnome who was about ready to go around the far turn of the road to eternity. Decades later I returned to the church and there—to my astonishment—he was, still poking his long wooden pole with its leather sock-like bag on the end in front of the attendees to entice donations. Apparently for him the road to eternity was very long.

While Rita was away for a few days with friends for a sightseeing tour of Vienna, I bought a long-haired Dachshund puppy. The children and I met Rita's returning train at the Heidelberg train depot and surprised her with the little fur ball in a cardboard box. I explained my logic for buying the dog by quoting comedian Robert Benchley, "A dog teaches a child fidelity, perseverance, and to turn around three times before lying down." We briefly named her Noodles and then changed her name to Peanuts, although Kathy amused herself by referring to the dog by the name she had read on her pedigree papers, Elena von der Schneider-Klauer. She became a good pal, sleeping mate, understanding confidante, and traveling mate to the children for the next fifteen years.

Kathy was ecstatic when there was a neighborhood children's animal parade. She gussied up Peanuts and entered her in the parade. She won a prize for her beauty and her costume. Rita loved to participate with the children in such affairs.

Germans love all animals, but are especially fond of dogs. An old lady said the only way she could safely cross a wide street or a city square and avoid being run down by aggressive motorists was to take her dog with her; no driver would ever harm a dog. Dogs were allowed in restaurants and most stores and public places. Grocery stores were an exception, but rings were provided outside for temporarily tying unhappy dogs while their owners shopped.

The German love of animals is even reflected in the language. German, much more than English, makes a clear and rigid distinction between formal, *sie* (you), and familiar, *du* (you). The familiar form is used with dogs and other animals. It is also used when speaking to God, family, children, lovers, and a handful of intimate friends. When old friends decide to switch from the formal to the informal form of speaking, it is usually with a serious ceremony such as a toast to *Bruderschaft* (brotherhood) while locking arms. Most of the time, the formal form is spoken. A company employee raised in the US in a rural German-speaking family and community only knew the familiar form. When he spoke to strangers in Germany, it was incomprehensible to them that he did not speak formally.

The kind of dog a person owns can be part of his persona. We had noted a tall, elegant young couple with a pair of stately white Saluki dogs on leashes who frequently walked around our neighborhood looking like a feature page out of a slick Hollywood movie star magazine. While having a haircut in a neighborhood barbershop on a Saturday morning, I thumbed through a typical barbershop tabloid magazine and saw a feature article about this very couple we had seen walking in front of our house. The article said they were in prison for fraud. Apparently as they paraded in a posh Baltic Sea resort hotel, a rich Texan took a shine to the head-snap beautiful female half of the couple and offered to "buy her" to take home. He paid them a substantial amount of money, but the couple skedaddled and he was unable to "take delivery" of his purchase. I couldn't wait to walk home to tell Rita about our glamorous, but notorious, neighborhood celebrities. We felt privileged to directly observe such a juicy event unfolding in our staid neighborhood.

Our Handschuhsheim neighborhood held a special celebration in 1967 to mark its thousand-year anniversary. There were speeches, parades, and marching bearded men dressed in animal hides and carrying clubs or spears on their shoulders. I was awed with the pageantry of the community as it celebrated its distant bygone times. I was even more awed when a local historian explained that the Celts and Romans previously occupied the area more than two thousand years before the age of Christianity. The surrounding farms and communities are strewn with Celtic artifacts and Roman building materials.

One of the most celebrated annual holidays in central and southern German was pre-Lenten *Fasching*—called Fat Tuesday, Carnival, or Mardi Gras in other countries. It was a time for rambunctious revelry, unrestrained behavior, elaborate parades, energetic dancing, masked balls, flamboyant costumes, exuberant singing, and unrestrained eating and drinking—all in preparation for the coming austerity of Lent during the forty days preceding Easter. Some of our best times were at costumed *Fasching* parties. Many say it is unwise to look too closely into the paternity of children born nine months after *Fasching* season.

May Day was the spring celebration in Germany for children. In our neighborhood, maypoles were erected with long streamers hanging down and flowers on the top. The children danced, sang, and walked around the poles in an intricate pattern as they braided the streamers together. In bigger communities, larger poles were erected with elaborately carved religious and historical scenes configured on long cross bars. The children also carried wooden May Day sticks with pointed ends. They impaled eight-inch-diameter soft pretzels on the points. Rita loved to learn the rituals and help the children participate in celebrations and holidays that were new to us.

It was sometimes a challenge for our daughter, Kathy, to live in Germany while she tenaciously held on to her American identity. Years later she reflected, "In the country of unlimited varieties of delicious wursts and mustards, I thought it a treat to go to the house of a friend with PX (US military store) privileges for buying Oscar Mayer baloney and French's yellow mustard. We used these precious ingredients to make sandwiches." She continued, "For years after returning to the US, I was the girl who was 'different' from my schoolmates."

By the time we returned home to the US, John had no American identity to hold onto. He brought his German identity home with him: he peed on the lawn (as little boys did in Germany); had to be told what window screens were for; tried to shake hands with his schoolmates each day; asked for his passport for travelling across the Mississippi River from Illinois to Iowa; insisted that roosters crowed *kickeriki* (not *cockle doodle doo*) and dogs barked, *vow vow* (not *bow wow*); and complained to his mother because she could not buy his favorite cheese, *quark* (a unique German cheese similar to American cottage cheese.)

It was years after returning home before the children stopped calling Rita *Mutti* (Mommy) and switched to Mom.

For a period of time in Germany, Kathy's proudest possession was her new Girl Scout dress. She wore it every day while we were on a two-week vacation in Yugoslavia. She would only remove it to change to her swimming suit for playing on the beach in front of our hotel.

Rita loved to work with the Girl Scouts from Kathy's school when they had camping outings. The US Army soldiers assisted by providing field toilets, water, stoves, tents, and security as if scouting events were military exercises.

Strictly enforced city regulations called for twice per year chimney cleaning by a certified *schornsteinfeger* (chimney sweep). Our sweeper came on a bicycle with his long-handled brushes and cleaning paraphernalia tied on a rack behind his bicycle seat. He wore a black stovepipe hat and black clothes as was traditional for his ancient and honored trade. According to tradition, children who touch chimney sweeps are assured of good luck for the coming months.

Rita liked the ceremony of their visits. When our young sweep went into our attic for chimney access, he commented on the outgrown children's toys. Rita gave the toys to him for his newborn son. It bonded their relationship. Some say the strict laws for chimney sweeping went into effect throughout Europe after a fire in a bakery on Pudding Lane started the Great London Fire of 1666.

Eating in Germany was a passion. If a restaurant served a bad meal, its continued existence was in jeopardy; Germans demanded quality food. American diners seldom found totally unfamiliar dishes on restaurant menus considering that many German foods are already known to them from the German immigrants to the US. Chefs prepared meals with meticulous attention to subtle spicing, quality ingredients, and attractive presentations. Waiters steered diners to the appropriate wines to complement the menu items. Eating in German restaurants was usually a special event and a joyous ceremony.

White asparagus, served with ham, butter, and new potatoes, was a favorite spring meal in southern Germany. The asparagus was grown under mounded soil so the sun did not turn the spears green. It is to vegetables what crocuses are to flowers—a harbinger of spring. We lived near the German asparagus capital, Schwetzingen, where the "noble stalk" is honored with an annual festival accompanied by concerts and theatrical performances. In the interest of not appearing boorish, I never admitted that I did not find white asparagus any tastier than the traditional green variety—but the accompanying festivities made it worthwhile.

A saying in Italy on eating could apply equally well in Germany: "One never grows old at the table."

Konditoreis, which were located in every neighborhood in Germany, Switzerland, and Austria, were like community institutions. They were similar to American coffee shops but on steroids. Brightly lit glass cases artistically displayed fresh pastries, cakes, strudels, fruits, nut breads, soups, ice cream, and the house specialties—a feast for the eye and nose as well as the mouth. The drink menus were long: coffee, tea, hot chocolate, sodas, wine, and beer. Konditoreis were the perfect place for morning or afternoon breaks with friends. For those without friends to chat with, there were racks of multilanguage newspapers mounted on sticks for easy holding and reading. At times Konditoreis looked like library reading rooms. Many customers also came to play games, write, and read at the small marble top tables. There is a saying in Vienna, "Time and space are consumed (in Konditoreis), but only the coffee is found on the bill." The shops varied from "holes in the wall" to finely designed rooms suitable for an emperor's sitting room. Homey service was always offered. In some Konditoreis on cold days, heat radiated from colorful, floor-to-ceiling glazed tile stoves set into the walls. Wet, cold dogs loved the decadent comfort provided by the stoves—and also a discrete offering from pastry plates.

In Germany, the community police set up small stations throughout cities. A single room on the ground floor of a house served our neighborhood. Although we never had need for police services, we felt that our property and family were quite secure because of their nearby presence.

Police cars and emergency vehicle sirens in Germany emit a sound unusual to American ears; phonetically, the sirens sound as if they are saying "dir-ty, dir-ty" in a rising tone. My children called them "dirty cars."

After my first year living in Germany, I discontinued working on Saturday mornings. We started the habit of making weekend visits to favored Heidelberg antique shops. The wartime necessity of selling items dug up from bombed building rubble or given up from troves of family heirlooms to barter for food and heating coal still lingered on. Fine items such as clocks, carved religious figures, and intricate chests were displayed in antiques shops and offered at affordable prices. The origin of some of the antiques was subject to dark speculation.

Our children found the visits to the antique shops endurable when the proprietors knew us better and started giving them treats and allowing them to play with their cats and dogs. They particularly favored Hermann, a large, lethargic, tan dog.

Although Kathy's schoolmates were primarily the children of GIs, civil service employees, and military support civilians, many had different backgrounds than were typical in the US. One of her friends who came to our house for play visits was Lucinda. She had an Asian/American GI father and a French mother. With her tilted red beret, flaring skirts, and dainty step, there was no doubting her French connection.

John often played at the home of his friend Renate, who was the daughter of a John Deere executive. John's continued welcome was dubious when he and Renate tried to saw off the leg of an antique wardrobe. Renate's house, which was a few blocks away, was big enough to be a hotel; in fact it was once a home for elderly people. It was built and occupied by Graf Ferdinand von Zeppelin, the famous inventor of lighter-than-air aircraft. After the mellowness that came from a few glasses of wine at the dinner table, those with active imaginations and a sense of history could imagine experimental model Zeppelins (dirigibles) swooping around the chandeliers under the thirteen-foot-high ceilings.

When I came home from work, two treats always awaited me: the excited greeting of our dog and the latest edition of the *New York Herald Tribune–Paris Edition*. In additon to news, the paper contained a column by American satirical journalist, Art Buchwald, who was a master of writing about naïve Americans in Europe and the French. He usually featured himself in his columns as a rustic boob.

One of his funnier articles was about traveling through a famous vineyard district of France. At the first stop, he gulped down a small glass of wine that was offered to him for tasting. His refined and well-connected companion explained how to swirl the wine around in his mouth to absorb the taste and aroma and then to spit it out on the dirt floor of the wine-aging cave or into a "spitting bucket." For the last stop of the day they visited the world-renowned Rothschild vineyard. They tasted the baron's finest wine in his luxurious oak-paneled library with valuable oriental rugs on the floor. For this last sampling, it was expected that the tasters would swallow the wine. Clueless Buchwald puckered up to spit out the costly wine after tasting it; it was implied that he was about to spit it on the precious carpet. In the closing line of the article, his friend screamed—but probably too late—"No! No! No!" Commenting on Buchwald's latest stories and quips was always suitable for conversation openers at cocktail parties.

Celebrating Christmas in Germany was not unlike in the US. The Germans originated decorating pine trees for Christmas, fanciful tree ornaments, and advent wreathes and calendars, "Silent Night" (actually written just across the border in Austria), and gingerbread houses. Christmas was a quiet, peaceful time. Lighting was mostly confined to subdued white giving the season an ethereal radiance.

It was a pleasure—but a very cold one—to visit the sprawling annual outdoor Kris Kringle Market in Nuremberg to buy Christmas items: decorations, trinkets, food, crafts, trees, gingerbread men and houses, wreathes, candles, candy, and carved nutcrackers. Rita's capacity for buying and cherishing more Christmas decorations was without limit.

We had our traditional family Christmas celebration on Christmas Eve in our home in Heidelberg. Then we called Rita's parents in the US; transatlantic phone calls were costly, infrequent, and brief.

Rita was raised in a household with loving but sometimes overly protective parents. She vowed that our children would be raised with fewer restrictions. When they wanted to buy treats, she put them alone on a streetcar—the narrow gauge interurban OEG—that passed a block from our house and sent them downtown to visit a favorite place, Horten Department Store. They liked to buy Danish Lego blocks (not yet widely available in the US).

Kathy tolerated John, who was four years her junior, because he spoke German and acted as her interpreter. Store clerks were accustomed to children acting as family interpreters. Many "guest workers" from Turkey, Greece, Spain, Yugoslavia, and Italy could not speak German, so their school-age children spoke for them in stores.

When Kathy was eight years old, she made her First Communion. We asked her what she would like for a present to celebrate the occasion. She answered, "Lunch at the Europäischer Hof Restaurant." The restaurant was in the most elegant hotel in the city. She wore her white First Communion dress and bridal wreath decorated veil. The professional wait staff and elite guests clucked over her as if she were a princess.

The finest evening dining ever for Rita and me was a *Silvesterabend* (New Year's Eve) dinner in 1965 also at the Europäischer Hof Hotel restaurant. The elegant old-world restaurant was the most excellent in Heidelberg. I dressed in my best blue suit and Rita in her finest cocktail dress and new mink stole that I gave her for a Christmas present. The formal dress of the restaurant staff rivaled that of the spit and polish of the British Cold Stream Guard (the Beefeaters) at morning inspection. The dining tables surrounded the intricately inlaid wood dance floor, and music was provided by a stringed ensemble playing classical and traditional folk music.

The evening dinner menu was written in the wide margins of a copy of a nineteenth century painting of university students with their colorful fraternity sashes while they drank, smoked, and ate at a table set up in the Heidelberg Castle courtyard. The fare for the evening was cold lobster from Helgoland; soup with truffles and goose livers; roast Virginia turkey with pineapple; cranberry sauce; French peas; artichokes; asparagus spears; tomatoes; potatoes; Brussels chicory salad; and, for desert, parfait "surprise" with wafers.

The end of the menu concluded with: *Silvester 1965—Unseren Gästen und Freunden wünschen wir ein glückliches, gutes und gesundes Neues Jahr—Prosit Neujahr 1966.* (New Year 1965—We wish our guests and friends good luck and a good and healthy New Year—A toast to the New Year, 1966.)

After the dinner, we eased our humble red VW out from the hotel parking lot full of haughty Mercedes, BMW, and Opel Senator cars—some with patiently waiting chauffeurs—and euphorically drove home. It was well worth using up most of our monthly entertainment budget for such a fine evening splurge. I framed the menu; it hangs to this day with our favorite pictures on our hall wall.

An American work colleague and his wife were often dinner guests at our house. They reciprocated by inviting us to be their guests in a Heidelberg restaurant. When I told Rita we would eat at the elegant Silbener Hirsch Restaurant across from the Holy Ghost Church on Market Square, she was delighted; it was one of her favorites. The leisurely dinner lasted for more than two hours giving ample time to enjoy each course and each wine. Our "old-world" waiter was attentive and competent. As we finished our meal, our American host said, "I apologize for bringing you to this crummy place: we wasted too much time between courses; our wine glasses were poured only half full; I had to scrape the "gravy" off my steak; and it took forever to get the bill. We should have been out of here in a half hour." On our short drive home Rita and I continued to savor our meal and recalled the biblical quotation about "not casting pearls before swine."

Rita and I were always uncomfortable when we heard such people disrespecting and mocking the local culture when it was different from ours. We sometimes shared remarks that we overheard from people who should never have left the corn and bean fields of their homes in the Midwest: They can speak English if they really want to. How much does that cost in 'real money' (US currency)? Why do they jabber so fast? The maid won't do things my way. (It was likely the first maid they ever had.) Why do they hold silverware in their left hand while eating? Why do they use that funny way to measure things (the metric system)? Why do they drive on the 'wrong side of the road' in Great Britain? We thought visitors had the right to observe but not to criticize.

Among our delightful acquaintances was Annette Fahramondi, a remarkably talented and beautiful woman, who was the young German wife of an Iranian doctor. She was an actress and a painter. We hired her to paint four oil pictures for us: a large portrait of Rita, Kathy, and John as they gazed at a sea shell; our children's favorite stuffed animals as seen through a thin veil as though the animals had become memories from the past; and two paintings of our children wearing traditional German costumes.

Frau Fahramondi moved to Iran with her husband and two children before the Shah was deposed and strict Islamic code was imposed. No further communication was ever again possible with her, and we feared for her welfare under the harsh new religious regime.

Because Rita handled most of our personal affairs, we had time in the evenings and weekends to discuss daily happenings, school meetings, neighborhood events, and the lives of Rita's friends, news from the US military community, German customs, Rita's daytime social life, and the activities of our children.

My work involved stress, pressure, and anxiety, but our home was always a sanctuary of calmness.

On most evenings after supper, talking, and putting the children to bed, I went to the office beside our bedroom and studied engineering drawings, correspondence, and work documents, or read nonwork related books. My office was furnished in massive walnut and red leather chairs and a well-used oriental rug—all from Rita's father's office when he retired. They overpowered the room, but they were free.

Our bedroom and the office had a connecting door. Rita went to bed early where she sat up reading her favorite mystery stories.

Near the end of our residence in Heidelberg, small groups of highly intelligent, left-wing political terrorists became active in Germany and elsewhere in Europe. One of the most noteworthy was the Red Army Faction—also called the Baader-Meinhof Group. They started a decades-long rampage of terrorism as student protesters by burning two Frankfurt stores. Their menu of issues and interests was long: the Vietnam War, communism, anarchy, anti-imperialism, anti-racism, women's liberation, and anti-capitalism. A Red Army Faction member justified its methods by explaining, "If one sets a car on fire, that is a criminal offence. If one sets hundreds of cars on fire, that is political action."

They attempted to achieve their objectives by assassinating officials, murdering capitalists (including the chairman of Daimler Benz), attempting to murder military authorities (they attempted to blow up the armored Mercedes carrying four-star US General Kroesen), arson, bank robbery, and masterminding court trials that would give them wide media coverage. Many of them died violently, often by suicide while in prison.

The Red Army Faction inspired radical groups to form in other countries around the world. It was not easy to understand why so many young people became too impatient to use the time-tested democratic processes to achieve their political objectives. However, we slowly began to comprehend there was a different generation walking on the streets, drinking in beer halls, and plotting and puffing in their "pads" with a new way of thinking.

Although The Red Army Faction eventually dwindled and collapsed, it haunted the West German and other European governments for decades.

Living in our quiet Heidelberg neighborhood when we were at the exuberant peak of our young adulthood was a fine way to enjoy life, absorb history, walk, raise children, strengthen our marriage, eat and drink, laugh, raise a dog, garden, visit antique shops, develop friendships, and awaken each day "rarin' to go."

I felt blessed; I had a beautiful, dynamic wife; healthy, normal children; a fulfilling professional life; adequate income; good health; and high hopes for the future. How good could life be?

Rita and Peanuts

Handschuhsheim Logo

John, Kathy, Rita, and the Red Bug

John's Birthday Party
Frank, John, Rita, and Kathy

Chimney Sweep

Painting
Kathy, Rita, and John

May Day
John and Kathy with Traditional Pretzel Sticks

CHAPTER 5

THE GERMAN PEOPLE

I have often felt a bitter sorrow at the thought of the German people who are so estimable as individuals and so wretched in groups.
—Goethe

Pandora Opening Her Box of Evils

The German people thought they had bet on the winning horse in 1934 when they allowed Adolph Hitler, with his ridiculous Chaplinesque mustache, to become their *Führer und Reichschancellor* (leader and chancellor.) But instead of the expected winning horse, the ill-fated Germans got the Four Horsemen of the Apocalypse as described in the

New Testament of the Bible. They symbolized pestilence, famine, war, and death. Each horseman would deliver its dreadful specialty in full measure during the next decade. Hitler's devilish leadership would wrap Germany in darkness and shame for decades.

The German people were taken in by Hitler's brilliant, mesmerizing oratory; gutter-level political skills; utter self-confidence; intention to unilaterally annul the harsh and unworkable post–World War I Versailles Peace Treaty; promise to end sky-high inflation; and assurance that industries would be revitalized and jobs restored. And his vicious harangues against the Jews and communists were readily accepted by many.

Hitler was a paradox. He looked like a funeral parlor embalmer—not the progeny of the blond, blue-eyed super race that he idolized. He was under-educated in a country that venerated learned people. He was born to unwed parents in another country (Austria.) With a résumé like this, his occupancy of the top government position seemed as strange as when loony Emperor Caligula allegedly gave his horse a seat in the Roman Senate.

It was hard to believe so many German people abandoned their hundreds of years of civilization, culture, sophistication, learning, and achievement and acted with the savage behavior of a wolf pack tearing into its prey.

Many people thought aggression was built into the German nature—especially the French. After the World War I Treaty of Versailles was signed, Marshall Foch, Commander of the Allied Forces, prophetically said, "This is no peace; it is an armistice for twenty years."

William L. Shirer, journalist and author of *The Rise and Fall of the Third Reich*, described the mindset of average German people in the early years of Hitler's reign:

> It was at this time, in the late summer of 1934, that I came to live and work in the Third Reich. There was much that impressed, puzzled, and troubled a foreign observer about the new Germany. The overwhelming majority of Germans did not seem to mind that their freedom had been taken away, that so much of their culture had been destroyed and replaced with a mindless barbarism, or that their life and work had become regimented to a degree never before experienced even by a people accustomed for generations to a great deal of regimentation. In the background, to be sure, there lurked the terror of the Gestapo and the fear of the concentration camp for those who got out of line or who had been communists or socialists, or too liberal or too

pacifist, or who were Jews. The Blood Purge of June 30, 1934 was a warning of how ruthless the new leaders could be. Yet the Nazi terror in the early years affected the lives of relatively few Germans and a newly arrived observer was somewhat surprised to see that the people of this country did not seem to feel that they were being cowed and held down by an unscrupulous and brutal dictatorship. On the contrary, they supported it with genuine enthusiasm. Somehow it imbued them with a new hope and a new confidence and an astonishing faith in the future.

But all of the German people—even the complacent ones—would soon become involved up to their necks as most of them willingly signed on to Hitler's agenda. For the next decade they would be governed by a grotesque, fanatical, unbalanced dictator who was a master of hatred, murder, terror, genocide, torture, and theft. Stefan George, a renowned German poet, called Hitler, "The Prince of Vermin."

The German people allowed monstrous abuse and extermination of their Jewish, Gypsy, Slav, elderly, handicapped, homosexual, Jehovah's Witnesses, and dissenter populations. In turn, they endured five million military and one to three million civilian deaths and the obliteration by bombing and shelling of most of their industrial cities. Some destroyed cities were "innocent bystanders" with no military or strategic value. Military historians sympathetic to the wanton destruction made it sound less savage by calling it "collateral damage."

Many people had to live for years in a postwar world as if they were animals going about their day-to-day lives in misery and desolation without adequate security, shelter, food, or clothing.

Hitler brought destruction to Europe on a scale not seen since the thirteenth century when Genghis Khan's thundering horde of Mongolian warrior-horsemen swooped in from the east bent on the genocide of all people who resisted his dominance. He boasted, "I am the flail of God!"

A handful of German people resisted Hitler at great personal peril. A future West German Chancellor, Konrad Adenauer, was on the run and for a short time a prisoner. Another younger future chancellor, Willy Brandt, fled to Norway, changed his name, and temporarily became a Norwegian citizen. They and others did not share the belief that all Germans should wear the mantle of collective guilt for the behavior of the Nazis.

Among the resolute anti-Nazis was Kurt Schumacher, a political leader who said in the Reichstag in 1932, "The Nazis appeal to the inner swine in human beings; they are unique in German history for their ability to mobilize human stupidity." For his impudence, he suffered and ruined his health in concentration camps for twelve years.

Another was Claus Graf von Stauffenberg, a Prussian Army officer and aristocrat, who participated in an aborted attempt to assassinate Hitler. He paid the supreme price when he fell in front of a firing squad. But he fared better than his older brother, a co-conspirator whom the Nazis slowly strangled—reputedly with a piano wire.

To think of Germany as a nation requires a short look at her history. The country is like a hobo soup; many ingredients were tossed in and the results were not always digestible and savory. Viewing the history of Germany from the earliest times reveals that it consists of a conglomeration of more than 1,700 mighty—as well as dinky—dukedoms, nations, city-states, principalities, and kingdoms.

With this mutt-like family tree, it is hard to understand how Hitler could have imagined that Germans and most Nordic people—excluding the groups that he despised and exterminated—were a race superior to all others.

Germany did not first become a united nation until 1870—only seven decades before Hitler's reign and less than a century before I lived in Heidelberg.

The complex mixture in Germany was made up of: (1) Lutherans in the north and Catholics in the south; (2) disciplined, militaristic Prussians and relaxed, fun-loving Bavarians; (3) a mishmash of civil codes; (4) rich, high-living Ruhr District industrial titans with slashed cheeks from dueling and frugal, hard-working Swabians; (5) schnapps sippers, wine connoisseurs, and beer guzzlers; and (6) dialect speakers who communicated in basically different languages.

In the stern north, a general was punished by death for disobeying an order even though his disobedience resulted in a great victory. In the south, when soldiers defied military orders that led to success, they received medals and honors.

Because of the mass immigration of Germans to the US in earlier times—often to avoid military conscription—German names are well-known even if the meaning of the words is not. German names are typically based on: occupations—Bauer (farmer); places—Hamburger (someone from Hamburg); animals—Katz (cat); or things—Nussbaum (nut tree). Some German names are longer and descriptive of a trade or deed: Eisenhower (iron hewer), Fenstermaker (window maker), and Manteuffel (man-devil.)

By the mid-1960s, when I moved to Germany, the memories of the Third Reich were rapidly fading. People were getting on with normal lives.

They were no longer hungry—a few were even overweight—but the fare for many was still basic. When I watched our factory workers eat their lunches in company cafeterias, I observed that their typical meal was a steaming bowl of thick potato and vegetable soup with a few morsels of meat. They ate it to the last tidbit and then wiped their bowls clean with bread scraps; they often topped it off with swigs of beer.

By the mid-1960s, ordinary people gave little thought to their recent history. Their bad memories of the war were stored away along with their worst nightmares. Their lives were mostly devoted to their mundane, day-to-day affairs: potholes in the roads, noise regulations in residential areas, and *schimpfen* (complaining) about the high taxes needed to support the expensive social programs that they had voted for.

I always wondered what each German I met was doing during the war. A few told me, but it was usually only after a long acquaintanceship.

While we lived in our quiet Heidelberg home, we had the opportunity to observe our new community and to note the contrasts to our previous neighbors in the US.

German people had a strong tie to the outdoors. They believed it nurtures good health. Fresh air was an obsession: windows were left open as much as possible; walking in the woods was popular; bedding and clothing were hung out for airing; and curative spas were identified by the quality of the surrounding air and the minerals in the water.

When patients were feeling poorly, their doctors often prescribed robust walks in the forests, meadows, and mountains. I visited a country spa where a high wooden lattice was built with mineral water flowing over it. The towel-wrapped patients sat downwind and breathed the moisture laden air. The spring water of each spa with its unique minerals was prescribed to provide relief for various ailments. It was easy to take full advantage of the generous socialized medicine system.

Spaziergang (walking) was a national passion—alone or in groups. The German people were lured to nature in a kind of mystical way. The countryside, forests, parks, and mountains were crowded with walkers and hikers on weekends. It is as if they were drawn back, like migrating animals, to the places where their pagan ancestors lived in the dark, medieval forests. The outings were usually planned with a rustic stopping place at the mid-point of the walk where light refreshments—beer, wine, pastries, or sandwiches—were served. Dogs often accompanied the walkers.

As I took a Sunday walk with my family and our dog on a tree-lined path overlooking the Neckar River, a purposeful group briskly tramped by. I had a vision of Richard Wagner's music thrumming in their ears with its theme of mythology, deep forests, heroics, mystery, drama, and Nordic, god-like people.

For city dwellers, walking the streets to window shop was popular. Store window decorating was a minor art form. Even though stores were never open on Sundays, the walkers could view the well-lit and attractive window displays and select future purchases.

Rita, our children, our dog, and I also liked to walk on Sundays. We favored flower gardens, river banks, quaint village streets, and the landscaped grounds of historical buildings. After a brief return home from our walks for a time-out, we regularly ate our suppers in small, neighborhood restaurants. Restaurant owners and waiters made guests feel especially welcome if they brought children or dogs for them to fuss over.

Shaking hands was far more prevalent in Germany than in the US. It was done on every business and social occasion by men, women, and children.

A foundry superintendent with whom I worked carried it to the limit even by local standards. Upon coming to work each morning, he went to the offices and desks of his employees, greeted them, and shook hands. Near the end of the workday he repeated the process.

When a large group of people attended a meeting and a late arrival came into the room, it would be disruptive for everyone to stand to shake hands. A shortcut protocol handled the problem: everyone rapped his knuckles on the table as a gesture in lieu of shaking hands.

I once embarrassed myself at a business/social affair by not knowing there was a protocol on the sequence of handshaking. I stuck my hand out to a company official who pointedly ignored me in favor of a more senior person.

Flowers were also a passion in Germany. Both men and women bought flowers, and most homes were decorated with fresh flowers each weekend. Substantial areas of cities and towns were devoted to much-enjoyed parks with well-tended flower beds; roses were a favorite. In early summer, rural road sides, fencerows, and ditches exploded with poppies as profusely as wild sunflowers in the US West.

It was not uncommon to see small tables set up on factory floors adorned with flowers—as well as an open bottle of wine—on workers' birthdays. Birthdays were always known and acknowledged in workplaces by fellow employees and managers.

In the spring, churches resembled funeral parlors at the wakes of important persons with pots and tubs decorated with large blooming branches from bushes and trees: forsythia, lilacs, honeysuckle, apples, cherries, crab apples, and plums.

When invited to German homes, it was the custom to bring flowers as a gift for the hostess. But the flowers were not to be presented in their wrappers; a never-solved problem was what to do with the wrapping paper at the last minute. The choices were to pocket the wadded-up paper or to toss it behind the bushes beside the door just before the hostess answered the doorbell.

In the mid-1960s, older German men typically dressed formally in dark suits, white shirts and ties, and felt hats when in public. The younger people were switching to more informal dress styles. When the older men tried to follow suit, it was not uncommon to see them make incremental steps, for instance changing to brightly colored polo shirts but leaving everything else the same. They looked as odd as the nineteenth century American Indians who topped their ornamental feathers and beads, buckskin trousers, and moccasins with black stovepipe hats when they traveled to Washington to meet the Great White Father.

The education system of Germany made a major split among students at an early age; those with promising grades, academic interests, and strong study habits attended gymnasiums (academic prep schools) and usually went on to earn university degrees. Those with lower grades or fewer academic interests followed a different track that could lead to apprenticeships, trade schools, or labor pools.

University students who earned PhDs were assured of an elevated social standing and access to high-level jobs in the civil service and private industry. Their status and prestige was second only to the aristocracy. In meetings where people with PhDs were present, they were always addressed as Herr or Frau Doktor and shown deference and respect.

In Germany, much attention was paid to the arts, particularly music. Cities commonly had opera companies, orchestras, and dance companies. Cultural institutions were generously funded with taxes. In nearby Mannheim, one of the more visible buildings is the National Theater, which was founded in 1779.

Carrying leather brief cases was common for most Germans. When workers carried them, Americans thought they were trying to make their neighbors think they worked at prestigious office jobs. Actually they used them to their carry lunches.

Hunting wild game in Germany was a popular sport; however, it was done with attention to strict training and rigidly controlled firearms permits. Hunters usually wore special green clothing and Tyrolean hats that evoked memories of childhood stories about gray-bearded European men in dark forests stalking wolves and deer. Hunting firearms could not contain more than two bullets.

The landowners controlled access to land and ownership of harvested game; they could keep the game, sell it to the hunters, or supply it to restaurants. Specialty restaurants served wild game. The cooks concentrated on cooking and spicing it to best enhance the game flavor.

Hunters often met in taverns to speak of their shooting exploits while sipping favorite drinks. Hunting was a ceremonial activity.

The Germans we encountered had a fine sense of humor, but it was often tuned to a different "funny bone" than that of Americans. I quit telling American jokes because they often fell flat.

German humor could have a wry quality to it: A man was walking his curly hair dog when a stranger asked, "Did you knit it yourself?"

Strong regional and dialect differences provided endless opportunities for ethnic jokes: "How many East Frisians (citizens of the northwest coastal region) does it take to milk a cow? Twenty-four—four to hold the teats and twenty to lift the cow up and down."

Individually the German people were considerate, friendly, and helpful. But their group behavior, by American standards, was sometimes less exemplary; they were pushy in public, aggressive while driving, harsh in judging the faults of others, and demanding that all rules be rigidly followed.

They furiously blinked their lights on the autobahns at motorists who drove for an instant too long in the left passing lane—horn blowing and passing on the right was forbidden. They became enraged at the slightest driving violation of other motorists and sometimes intimidated the transgressors by driving too close and sharply cutting in front.

The superb autobahns between cities were without speed limits. The feeling of speed was intensified because, with the high land values, the highways have narrow median strips and shoulders and sharp entry and exit ramps. Some motorists drove more than one hundred miles per hour. When there was an accident at such speeds, the consequences were often gruesome.

German traffic laws were precisely written and rigidly obeyed. More casual American drivers could expect vigorous "finger waggling" and stern, angry lectures if they were less rigorous in adhering to the traffic laws. On the other hand, Americans often stood out by courteously giving way to other motorists at stop signs and in heavy traffic.

Adherence to rules and customs was followed in other areas as well. A neighbor was asked to stop washing his car on weekends because visible Sunday work was not allowed.

Another neighbor rang our doorbell on a Sunday morning to complain that the night before he heard audible talking when I accompanied my departing guest to his car at the curb.

After we learned and respected the local rules and customs, we enjoyed friendly and tranquil relationships with our neighbors, work colleagues, and social acquaintances.

Nazi Rally—1939

The Four Horsemen of the Apocalypse
Pestilence, Famine, War, and Death

CHAPTER 6

THE KONRAD ADENAUER ERA
1949 to 1963

The problems of victory are more agreeable than those of defeat, but they are no less difficult.
—Winston Churchill

Konrad Adenauer

Ludwig Erhard was the Chancellor (Prime Minister) of West Germany during the time we lived in Heidelberg. But it is not possible to understand and appreciate the Erhard era without first understanding the previous turbulent thirteen years of the Chancellor Konrad Adenauer era.

The problems faced by seventy-three-year old Adenauer when he became the first chancellor of prostrate, postwar West Germany rivaled those of Mother Hubbard and her empty cupboard. Every dog in Germany was now in urgent need of a bone—as well as shelter, clothing, medical care, and employment. The citizens were demoralized, confused, dispirited, uncertain, and exhausted. They felt like they were descending in a vortex with nothing to hold onto.

It was humbling and humiliating for the Germans to have to live in postwar poverty and misery after decades of enjoying one of the highest living standards in the world. Part of their previous high standard came from the backs of the people in colonized or conquered territories that were now lost to them. It was also hard for them to come to grips with the realization that most of their vaunted Nazi governrnent officials could be the cast for a horror movie.

The collapse and capitulation of Fascist Germany ended with the signing of an unconditional surrender on May 8, 1945 in the presence of the victorious Allied Forces. The celebrated Nazi Third Reich, which proclaimed that it would reign in glory for a thousand years, toppled into the dump in a little more than a decade. All of Germany lay desperate and miserable with the vengeful Russian bear to the east; the exhausted British lion and jubilant American eagle to the west; and the conceited French rooster trying to find any opening to snatch a few pecks from the German carcass.

The triumph of victory in Europe by the Allied Forces after six years of war and 40 million deaths immediately gave way to conflicts, uncertainties, instability, tension, and confusion. The clarity of purpose among the Allied Forces while defeating Nazi Germany ended. The power centers in Moscow, London, Washington, and Paris staged countless inconclusive conferences with each other—and sometimes even within the walls of their own council chambers. Students of European history recalled the similarity to the multination Thirty Years War where, for decades, uncompromising European adversaries could not find common grounds for coexistence.

After the war ended in 1945, it was the beginning of a round of unspeakable misery, suffering, and often death for the ethnic Germans who were forced to abandon their homes, businesses, and land in the East: Poland, Czechoslovakia, Yugoslavia, Russia, Hungary, Romania, the Baltic countries and former eastern territories of Germany. Some had lived in these countries and locations for so long that they had absorbed the local cultures and lost their ability to speak German. Most were dumped into Germany with no place to live and no way to survive. I worked with some of the displaced persons. By their accents I could easily tell the German language was not their mother tongue.

Over a period of five years, fifteen million persons of German ancestry from the east were coerced to trek west to the four occupied zones of war-torn, chaotic Germany where people already were hungry and starving and living in tents, barns, shacks, barracks, haystacks, camps, cellars, fields, and on the streets. The refugee flow became a flood of bewildered people who came in appalling misery; for many it was a death march.

There were many reasons for the unprecedented pell-mell migration and deportation of refugees: enforcement of the secret deals made by the leaders of the war victors (Stalin, Roosevelt, and Churchill), dread of the Russians, revenge, nationalism, property grabbing, ethnic cleansing, jealousy, hatred, and fear. Stalin cynically believed that so many people dumped on top of desperate Germany would destabilize the country and soften it up for communist domination.

Some of the persuasive and effective methods for inducing ethnic Germans to move west were rape, murder, intimidation, arbitrary arrests, detention, torture, confinement, and property destruction. Stalin advised the Red Army and legions of accompanying Russian officials, "Create such conditions for the German that they will want to escape from the East."

Rape of German women on a massive scale—primarily by Russian soldiers—was one of the most searing atrocities; many abused victims never recovered. The Red Army regarded captured territories—especially in Germany—a mammoth brothel with all of the cash registers disconnected. The population of occupied German territory was predominantly female. Most men were in the military, in prison, or dead; few were around to help protect women from the vengeful Red Army. When Stalin was asked to subdue the rampant raping and plundering by his army, he said, "Considering the hardships the Russian soldiers and citizens endured because of the Germans earlier in the war, I think our soldiers earned the right to take a little pleasure with their women and pilfer a few of their trinkets for souvenirs."

For many of the deportees, the forced trip west to Germany was like running a gauntlet. Up to two million died in the deadly exodus. They walked, crawled, or rode in wagons, in buggies, in open railroad cars, in the back of trucks, on horseback, and on the backs of relatives. A sorry, miserable lot they were!

Deportees were often called "displaced persons" or "DPs." Considering the dire condition of Germany after the war, some of the DPs moved on past Germany to other countries including the US.

Historians sometimes compare this exodus to our blotted history book pages during the "Trail of Tears" incidents in the 1830s when 45,000 Native Americans from various tribes tribes—Cherokee, Creek, Seminole, Chickasaw, and Choctaw—were forced by the US government to move from their traditional southeastern tribal territories to scruffy reservations in the far off west. Many starved, froze, and died on the trail. Alexis de Tocqueville, a French thinker and historian, wrote of the event:

> In the whole scene there was an air of ruin and destruction, something which betrayed a final and irrevocable adieu; one couldn't watch without feeling one's heart wrung.

De Tocqueville's words foretold the miseries of the European exodus a century later and proved the ancient adage about history repeating itself.

Heartbreaking uncertainties and questions would haunt the DPs—as well as other disrupted Germans—for years: Were their loved ones still alive but in Siberian labor camps? Did they die in battle? Were they alive but unable to communicate? Thousands of messages were posted on bulletin boards begging for information about lost relatives and friends.

The uprooting and abuse of so many Europeans was a catastrophe. Those who survived the unprecedented flight desperately longed for security and the restoration of a feeling of self-worth.

Along with the exodus, national borders were moved—especially in doomed Poland. The cynical border manipulation and territory grabs during and after the war recalled the Biblical story about the Roman soldiers casting lots for the distribution of Jesus' garments when he was crucified.

The hapless Germans would continue to suffer—even though the war was over—for years until the Allies reached an uneasy détente among themselves and charted the fate of defeated and divided Germany. East Germany—under the harsh heel of communist Russia—and West Germany—subject to the stern and demanding wishes of Great Britain, the US, and France—would take distinctly different roads to the future.

After the former Allies—Russia and the Western Powers—finally accepted that they had no choice but to co-exist with their fundamentally different political philosophies and forms of governing, the two Germanys could take their first uncertain steps toward political and economic recovery.

Strategic political thinkers were not entirely unhappy with a divided Germany; it would reduce the possibility of a resurgent group of Nazis again becoming a military threat. John Foster Dulles, the US Secretary of State, privately said to President Eisenhower, "There's a great deal to be said for the status quo" (a divided Germany).

In 1949 after the occupying Western Powers granted partial sovereignty to West Germany, Konrad Adenauer, a seventy-three-year-old lawyer, wily politician, student of German history, and statesman, became the first chancellor of the Federal Republic of Germany—commonly called

West Germany. He had the seemingly hopeless job of rebuilding the mess left to him after twelve years of rule by the Nazi "Thousand-Year-Reich." Because of his age he was nicknamed *Der Alte* (the old one). He was thought to be a caretaker leader, but for the next decade and a half, he would competently lead his tattered country—populated by the most ostracized people on earth—down a long, treacherous road to democracy, freedom, capitalism, prosperity, stability, and finally respectability and integration with the other western countries.

Adenauer recognized that for a time he would need to wear the shroud of social pariahhood for the German people. And he understood that what soon would become West Germany had no chance at all of surviving and rebuilding without the protecting US military umbrella garrisoned in Germany and the support of the policymakers in Washington.

Adenauer's towering moral stature; his calm self-assurance; his unshakable faith in Christianity, Western culture, and democracy; his support of people's right to property ownership—but not of cartels and monopolies; and his nearly flawless ability to correctly see the German situation in a light seen by only a few others made it hard to imagine anyone else as Chancellor.

He was a steadfast member of the CDU (Christian Democratic Union) party, a center-right organization that supported a free-market economy, social welfare programs, and European integration.

Although Adenauer was a staunch Roman Catholic, he formed a government that was also inclusive of other faiths. Churches were not only for religious purposes in Germany; they were directly associated with political parties and the general culture. The shadows of the devastating Thirty Years War in the 1600s where the Catholics and Protestants duked it out in bloody and bitter battles for supremacy still fell across Germany and Europe.

Adenauer knew how to define the issues that were important to postwar Germans: stability, security, and respectability; social and moral reforms; needs of single parents; needs of homeless and destitute families; and avoidance of a rigid, doctrinaire position on the radical dogmas of either right or left politics. He understood the German people's deep longing for the chance to lead normal lives and forget the utter and humiliating failure of the grandiose ventures of the recent past.

But Adenauer's grandfatherly image concealed another part of his character; he practiced the chancellor's role with the manipulative guile of Nicolai Machiavelli and the Texas bar fight subtlety of Lyndon Johnson. A few said the stage upon which Adenauer performed was too small to fully utilize the full range of his unbounded capabilities.

Adenauer's job was not made any easier because of the weak and inconsistent governing of Germany by the occupying Western Powers during the first four postwar years.

The long list of difficulties and issues that Adenauer faced seemed to be overwhelming. This chapter will only speak of a few of the most complex and persistent problems.

One of his first decisions was to locate the capital of West Germany in ancient Bonn on the Rhine River instead of larger Frankfurt or Hamburg. Adenauer thought selecting Bonn emphasized that the capital was temporary until Germany reunited and it could be reestablished in Berlin. To many, this hope seemed futile.

He also knew that too much emphasis on reunification of East and West Germany and reestablishing Berlin as the capital would not go over well with the war victors. He must temporarily shroud his never-ceasing desire for reestablishing the prewar geographical status of a reunified Germany.

Crafty Adenauer accepted the temporary division of West Germany and East Germany until red-hot wartime emotions cooled down. As long as the separation went on, the neighboring countries would think Germany was harmless and they were secure from her next war of conquest. He knew that many who were so grievously harmed by the Nazis now viewed Germany like a trussed up rogue elephant. The overwhelming fear was that if the beast were unshackled, she would again go on an elephant-like rampage because that was the animal's nature.

Adenauer's lifelong study of German political history served him well while he was chancellor. He understood the complex history of the Germanic people. It was like a very old house with countless layers of paint. Each layer had a story to tell and each influenced subsequent layers.

Adenauer would bide his time until fears faded and his countrymen proved they could "play nicely with her neighbors." In his crystal ball, he could foresee the time when the economic model of large industrialized West Germany—eventually reunited with smaller agrarian East Germany—would peacefully dominate Europe without the need for military force.

I once wrote the term "West Germany" in a John Deere company document. A trusted and respected German colleague asked me to change it to "Germany." He wanted to emphasize, in his own small way, that the reunification of West Germany and East Germany would eventually occur.

West Germany was cut off from her traditional breadbasket in East Germany and Eastern Europe. At first, the occupying Western Powers would not permit West Germany to rebuild her factories and export markets. Without export income from industrial production, there was no way for West Germany to pay for essential food imports. Soon after Adenauer came to power, the Western Allies relaxed their policy on industrial rebuilding.

Recovery then proceeded swiftly and the problems of unemployment, housing, hunger, and starvation diminished. In 1950 food rationing ended. Many of the skilled people needed for planning, rebuilding, and managing in the postwar era were still around; they were the same people who had recently built the massive, technically advanced arsenal for the Third Reich. The industrial complex of Germany remained largely hands-off to the Nazis during the war. The postwar industrialists only needed to retool but this time for peaceful intentions.

One of the thorniest and most persistent issues for West Germany and the Western Allies was the denazification process—cleansing the stained fabric of German culture of every shred of Nazism and punishing the criminally guilty.

It was a lengthy, messy, and emotionally bruising process that had to consider morality, conflicting legal systems, revenge, propaganda, war crimes, justice, amnesty, blame, and the ever-present shadow of politics.

The Nuremberg Trials were established to try high-ranking Nazi officers and to set up a bureaucratic process to determine which individual Nazis and German people were responsible for the crimes of World War II in Europe. And to make it more difficult, there was the simultaneous turmoil of Germany splitting into two countries and the intensifying collision between the controlled economy and society of Russia and the capitalist economy and culture of the US.

Few had the skill necessary to lead West Germany through this quagmire. Most historians would later agree that Germany and the US had excellent people to lead the task—Konrad Adenauer as the German Chancellor and John McCloy as the US High Commissioner. McCloy, a lawyer, diplomat, and business executive, had the task of creating a civilian government in West Germany after four postwar years of military rule and rebuilding its industry and commerce.

McCloy succeeded the US military commander, General Lucius Clay. Adenauer and McCloy had the diplomatic and political skill and wisdom to work together to restructure West Germany and bring her back into the community of civilized and respected nations.

Die Zeit wrote that McCloy was the conscience of America. Richard Weizsächer, president of West Germany, said he was the Godfather of Germany. *Harper's* wrote that he was the most influential private citizen in America. This was indeed high praise considering the perils infesting the churning waters that McCloy swam in: uncertainty, suspicion, fear, regret, despair, grief, guilt, hopelessness, betrayal, and disenchantment with traditional values. He helped the evolving German government close the lid on Pandora's box of evils that the Nazis had opened.

Many in the victorious Western Powers at first took tough positions on defeated Germany: The Germans must rebuild what they destroyed. None of the ex-Nazi leaders should be allowed in the new postwar government. The German wartime military was profoundly evil and should be permanently crippled. Rebuilding the industrial economy of Germany would lead to the next war of conquest. John McCloy was too soft on the Germans—he was granting amnesty to too many people. All of the German people should wear the mantle of guilt for the war; they should recognize and admit their moral bankruptcy. And the Germans should gratefully accept the US as their liberator from the evil forces of the Third Reich. But these positions were not universally accepted by a long shot.

US public opinion against Germany was especially hardened when the horrors of the concentration camps became widely known and it was revealed that eighty captured American soldiers were shot in the back of the head by German soldiers at Malmedy, Belgium, during the Battle of the Bulge—the last hope for the German Army to stop the advancing Western Allied Forces.

McCloy said, "Although I have the power of a dictator, I wield it with a gentle hand. We neither buy allies nor force anyone to be our partners." Some Germans challenged this judgment.

Adenauer said, "In view of the confused times behind us, a clean slate is now called for. Pursuing politically exonerated and noncriminal persons should end. It is time to stop 'sniffing out' Nazis."

Even General Eisenhower's towering rage when he saw the German atrocities committed in the concentration camps subsided when he later said, "There is a real difference between the regular soldiers and officers and Hitler and his criminal group. The fact that certain individuals committed dishonorable and despicable acts reflects on the individuals and not on the great majority" and "The German soldier fought bravely and honorably for his homeland."

By the 1950s most top German and US officials tacitly agreed that no further purpose would be served by continuing to arouse the dogs of national memory with more trials.

The Russians governed by making meticulous, detailed plans for every aspect of the economies, governments, and private lives of citizens in countries where they ruled or wished to rule. The plans were accompanied by iron-fisted enforcement police.

Phase one of the Russian plan for communizing Western Europe was to dislodge the Western Allies—the US, Great Britain, and France—from Berlin followed by a takeover of all of Germany and eventually all of Europe. Molotov, the Russian foreign minister, explained it clearly when he said, "Whoever controls Berlin controls Germany and whoever controls Germany controls Europe."

The Russians feared—with justification—that if the West had a foothold in Berlin, it would provide an opportunity for spying, radio broadcasting, and opening a "hole in the fence" for people to escape from the East to the West.

In 1948 the Russians cut off ground access to the non–Russian-controlled sectors of Berlin. The Western Allies responded by initiating the massive and costly Berlin airlift to supply the beleaguered Berliners with their essential needs. For a year they delivered up to five thousand tons per day of coal, clothing, food, equipment, and medical supplies. In 1948, the humiliated and embarrassed Russians reopened ground access to the city when Western forces were not dislodged as they expected.

The humanitarian airlift started to soften the negative West German attitude that the 150,000 occupying US soldiers were an unwelcome force. They realized they would be totally at the mercy of Russia if the US forces withdrew. When the airlift pilots started dropping candy and treats to the besieged children during their Berlin landing approaches, it helped mollify hardened hearts. And the harshness of US troops' treatment of Germans started to diminish by the time of the airlift; the battle-hardened troops were now being replaced by new less-hostile soldiers who had not experienced the horrors and atrocities of war.

From the vantage point of a half century later, when I look back and remember that uncertainty existed in the 1960s about who would win the Cold War, it seems that it should have been obvious that the West would win. But at the end of the war, some thought of capitalism as the system that supported the German Nazis and the Italian Fascists. Communism appealed to many as the better system of government.

Molotov, the Russian foreign minister, was more clear-sighted; he understood that if the Germans were ever allowed to have free elections, Russia would be the loser. He knew the Russian-style, rigged elections were a farce.

Also uncertain was whether or not the US was firmly committed to militarily and economically sticking it out in postwar Germany and Europe. Many in the US said, "The war is over; let's demobilize our armed forces and keep our nose out of foreign affairs." There was a great fear in West Germany that she would need to stand alone to face Russia.

Without a sound currency, the powerful West German Deutschmark, the fast rebuilding of a robust industrial and commercial economy could not have happened. The father of the robust economy was portly, scholarly, cigar-chomping Ludwig Erhard.

Adenauer accepted Erhard's learned and pragmatic leadership for the economy, but he feared that he might someday be a contender for the chancellor's job. He thought Erhard had inadequate political experience and passion for the job. Adenauer's studious reading of all memos and position papers, sending spies into his ministers' offices, and micromanaging his staff was in total contrast to Erhard's easy-going, trusting style. Erhard thought most people were fundamentally good and he need only define broad principles to his staff and they would do the right thing on their own. His style did not always go down well with his staff; they were accustomed to top-down orders given by strong political bosses. Adenauer did everything he could to shamelessly discredit Erhard personally and professionally. He only kept him as his top economic minister because of his vaunted reputation for having spearheaded Germany's lightning-fast economic recovery after the war.

Chancellor Adenauer and High Commissioner McCloy had the wisdom to sweep a lot of nasty stuff under the rug away from continued public view in order to move ahead in building a new West German society.

By 1952 most of the war crime problems and exoneration and reintegration issues were resolved—or buried—and the emerging and developing government could concentrate on the long list of other urgent situations and difficulties.

In 1953 East Germany rose up against her Russian occupiers. For West Germans, watching the East German uprising against her communist government and the brutal Russian military retaliation was like living behind the banks of a raging river and hoping the dikes would hold and keep the waters in check. Most German people had a visceral fear of the ruthless and unpredictable behavior of the Russians: Would they cut off Berlin again? Would they menace or attack West Germany? Could fledgling NATO and the US be relied upon to defend West Germany against the Russians? After the East German uprising, the Adenauer government reassessed its policies on refugees, rebuilding her army, her role in NATO, and her relationships with the Western occupying powers. It became clear that the Russian bear had sharp teeth and would use them. A powerful counterforce would be needed.

In 1954 a sports event lifted the spirits of the West German people when they unexpectedly won the prestigious football World Cup. The acclaim for their victory was enormous. It was as if they finally received a pat on the head after being allowed out of the dog house of negative world opinion for the first time in a decade.

NATO limped along like a paper tiger until 1950 when the Korean War started. After Germany became a member in 1955, she soon became a serious part of NATO and contributed to it becoming a deterrent to Russia's challenge and threat to Western Europe.

When West Germany built up her military, it helped her gain standing as a country that could handle her own security. She became a partner with her occupying Western Allied Forces, and she started to acquire stature as a civilized and respected world citizen.

Those who opposed the Nuremberg war criminal trials could now say, "I told you so. The German army that was judged to be fundamentally evil during the trials now needs to rearm to counter the growing threat of the Russian Red Army."

Berlin was a constant point of contention between Russia and the West. Khrushchev, in his rustic fashion, said, "Berlin is the testicle of the West. When I want the West to scream, I squeeze Berlin."

East Germany and Russia had to stop the mass exodus of skilled and educated people from East to West Germany. East Germany could not run her economy and government without competent managers and professionals. Her clumsy solution to stop the flood of fleeing people was to build one of the world's greatest eyesores—the Berlin Wall. The obvious solution—reform the government and the economy—was as impossible for the communists as it would be for a zebra to change its stripes to polka dots. The wall became Russia's dunce cap for showing the world that communism was a failed form of government.

At an earlier time, John Kennedy and Konrad Adenauer had little respect for each other. Adenauer thought Kennedy was "naïve and undisciplined." Kennedy said Adenauer was "a relic of the past and too old for any kind of workable relationship."

When Kennedy gave his *Ich bin ein Berliner* (I am a citizen of Berlin) speech in Berlin, it gave hope to the Berliners, electrified the German people, and served notice to the Russians that the US was deeply rooted in West Germany. And it proved to Adenauer that Kennedy had acquired political chops and it reduced his fear that the U.S would not steadfastly support West Germany in the face of a Russian showdown.

Fortunately, memories are short; by then most had forgotten the Kennedy administration's role in the bungled and failed Cuban invasion. Later when the embarrassing mess was reviewed, Kennedy bitterly said, "The first advice I'm going to give my successor is to watch the generals and to avoid feeling that because they were military men their opinions on military matters were worth a damn."

Adenauer said. "…unspeakable crimes have been committed (against the Jews) and they demand restitution, both moral and material…"

He knew anything West Germany did directly to mitigate the Nazi atrocities committed against the European Jewish community and to pay for the confiscation of Jewish property would be like touching the third rail in a subway. It was extremely hard for many Israelis to accept the aid offered to them by Germany because they thought of it as blood money being paid to help Germany regain international respectability. Some classical scholars in Israel recalled the warning given in Virgil's writings, "I am wary of (treacherous) Greeks, even those bearing gifts."

Over several decades, Germany quietly made massive payments to fledgling Israel to help build her economy, knowing, however, it would never be adequate penance for the searing horrors of the Holocaust. In fact, one of the biggest items in the West German national budget was the hefty amount for reparations to Israel for the victims of Nazi atrocities—more than 100 billion Deutschmarks ($25 billion in US currency) over the years.

"Made in Germany" was stamped on railroads, telephones, docks, ships, irrigation systems and entire areas of industry and agriculture that West Germany shipped to Israel. The West German aid played an important role in building the infrastructure and economy of the new state of Israel. Adenauer neither expected forgiveness for the behavior of the Nazis toward the Jews nor public acknowledgment of German aid to Israel.

For years, Jews around the world would not buy German-made products. However, by the 1960s, partly due to the reparations paid by Germany to Israel, Jews started to buy Mercedes and Volkswagen cars.

After 1952 a new slate of problems occupied the postwar West German government.

The Adenauer government suffered severely over "The Spiegel Scandal." *Der Spiegel* (the *Time Magazine* of Germany) published an article claiming the newly formed West German Army was only prepared for battle to a 'limited rating'—the lowest NATO grade. Franz Strauss, minister of defense, accused *Der Spiegel* of treason and illegally shut down the magazine. Based on proof that Strauss lied to parliament about his role in the scandal, he was sacked. Adenauer became politically involved and was forced to reorganize his government.

One of the last actions during the Adenauer era was the signing of a treaty with haughty and prickly Charles de Gaulle, the towering six-foot five-inch president of France. It was a seminal achievement considering Germany and France's centuries-long history of wars, betrayals, retribution, contempt, and distrust. Lasting peace with Germany was part of de Gaulle's grand vision for reestablishing the grandeur and glory of France. To the surprise of many, it would be a durable treaty that would establish a strong foundation for future economic, military, administrative, trade, and monetary unification between France and West Germany and many other Western European countries.

De Gaulle's vision also included development of French weapons, withdrawal from NATO, and policies independent of the US and Great Britain. When de Gaulle tilted up his ample Gallic nose and repeatedly uttered his standard "*non*" answer to outside proposals, it exasperated and perplexed those who dealt with him.

When Adenauer resigned as chancellor at eighty-two, he enjoyed the remaining four years of his life knowing his leadership had transformed West Germany from being the reviled pariah of the world to a country of stability and respectability.

Adenauer left the political stage just before I moved to Germany. It seemed strange to read newspaper articles about central Europe that were no longer dominated with stories about *der Alte*.

Adenauer's modest deathbed words—spoken to his daughter in his native Cologne dialect—summed up his feelings of contentment with his long life and his satisfaction with the condition and status of West Germany: *Da jitt et nix zo kriesche* (There's nothing to squawk about!).

The West Germany that my family lived in for the next four years was a stable and enduring national structure created through the leadership of Konrad Adenauer and based on the economic underpinnings conceived and executed by Ludwig Erhard.

Berlin in Ruins

Divided Berlin
1948

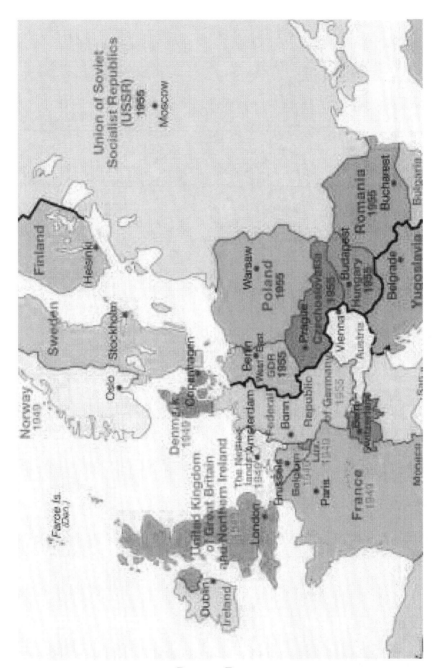

Postwar Europe

German President Lübke, US High Commissioner McCloy, and Chancellor Adenauer

President Eisenhower and Chancellor Adenauer

CHAPTER 7

BUILDING AN IRON FOUNDRY IN MANNHEIM

When man wrested iron from the earth
The earth would never again be the same

Pouring Molten Iron into a Mold

Iron foundries melt scrap metal and pig iron for pouring into sand molds—similar to pouring melted chocolate into Easter bunny molds. Factories then finish and assemble the iron castings into engines, transmissions, tractors, cars, and a list of other products as long as a child's Christmas wish list.

Making iron castings is a gritty business carried out in an environment of sand and fine coal dust, high temperatures, unpleasant odors, deafening noise, and significant danger. And yet the work must be done with a high degree of skill and precision.

The John Deere foundry in Mannheim, as it stood in the old Lanz factory, produced iron castings for all of the John Deere European factories. It was obsolete and dingy; it had limited capability for delivering the precision castings required for manufacturing diesel motors and modern farm equipment.

Each morning for three years, I set off from my Heidelberg home to manage the complete rebuilding of the Mannheim foundry. Simultaneously with the foundry project, other teams were redesigning and rebuilding the adjacent tractor factory.

Plans for the complete redesign and expansion of the foundry were made in John Deere's central manufacturing engineering offices in Moline, Illinois, and the board of directors appropriated the required funds.

It was my assignment to convert the foundry plans to German standards and environmental regulations; locate and evaluate equipment suppliers; contract for and install the new equipment; supervise the contractors' work; approve payments; control the budget; maintain the schedule; and arbitrate conflicts between US and German engineering methods and business practices.

We set up our offices on the second floor of the existing Mannheim foundry office building with a staff of nine—three engineers (a Hollander, a German, and an Australian), two technicians, a purchasing agent, an interpreter/translator, and two bilingual secretaries—along with temporary visiting engineers from the US.

We worked well together as a team in a casual but professional environment. When we spoke English we addressed each other by our first names in the American manner. When speaking German we addressed each other formally: *Herr, Frau, and Fräulein.*

The modernization and expansion was done while production continued in the existing foundry. This was akin to changing running shoes while in the middle of a foot race. There were frequent conflicts—even an occasional shoving match and fist fight—between the production and hired construction contractor employees.

Four people tragically lost their lives during the foundry construction: Two fell from heights to the concrete floor, one breathed lethal furnace gas, and one was crushed in a casting finishing machine. While all the deaths were dreadful, the most heart-breaking was of a young man who had just escaped from an oppressive Eastern European country to establish a new and better life for his family in West Germany.

Germany and Switzerland were centers for the thriving iron foundry and steel industries of Europe. It was not difficult to find experienced foundry equipment contractors willing to aggressively compete for orders.

In order to evaluate potential foundry equipment suppliers and to monitor and approve their work after they were awarded contracts, my colleagues and I traveled extensively to industrial locations throughout West Germany and to several other countries.

Although most of the industrial rebuilding after the wartime bombing and artillery destruction of West Germany was over, extensive evidence remained of the shortcuts taken to rapidly get Germany and other war-torn countries back on their feet. The John Deere factory still clearly showed the effects of bombing: partially rebuilt walls, foundations of destroyed buildings, empty spaces, raw open basements, and patched-up walls.

In the interest of economy, many other multistory buildings elsewhere in Germany had "Paternoster" elevators. The passenger compartments of the elevators continuously moved so that to step on and off took the agility of a child playing hopscotch. The elevators were named after the first two words in Latin of the "Our Father" prayer as recited in the rosary, because the passenger platforms were imagined to be like rosary beads. They were later replaced with conventional, safer elevators that stopped at each floor.

I visited a small town in the north on an exceedingly cold winter day to examine a foundry dust control system. In the morning, I tip-toed across the icy floor to the lavatory in my unheated hotel room with the expectation of warm water for washing—a common toilet was down the hall. The lavatory had only a cold water tap, but a device that looked like a cattle branding iron with an electric cord lay on the basin ledge. With uneasiness about electrocution, I tentatively stuck the device in the basin and waited for it to heat the water. The cold, primitive hotel room took me back to the days in my unheated childhood bedroom on a South Dakota farm. Hot running water and central heating would need to wait for the next stage of postwar rebuilding.

We hired an engineering company in Zurich, Switzerland, to convert US foundry designs to German standards. The German Industrial Standards (DIN standards) were so comprehensive that they also became the standards for other European countries.

Every two weeks I rode a train from Mannheim to Zurich—a two-hour trip—to direct and approve the work undertaken by the engineering company. I soon learned the Swiss were an orderly and self-confident people. A colleague told me they considered the design of roads, bridges, factories, and buildings in other countries to be only minimally acceptable in Switzerland. They exceeded normal design standards to make their structures and factories the best in the world, and they did not always conceal their smugness about their real—but sometimes imaginary—superiority.

An unsettling hotel routine in Switzerland, as well as in many other Eurpean countries, was the desk clerk's demand to hold guest passports for the night so they would available for police inspection. Although it was scary to be deprived of passports, they were always meticulously returned to guests the next morning. The reason for police inspection was not obvious.

A European custom that seemed quaint to American visitors was setting shoes in the hotel hall for cleaning and shining by the hall porter during the night. After Konrad Adenauer became the chancellor of postwar West Germany, he made his first trip to Washington with the assumption that the US hotels had the same custom. However, when he placed his shoes outside his hotel room for shining, they were taken.

Nicolas Hayek, a Swiss citizen of American and Lebanese origin, owned the engineering firm, Hayek Engineering, that we hired in Zurich to assist us with our foundry project. Hayek was a consummate businessman and diplomat with the acute intelligence and the silky savvy of a camel merchant in a tented Saharan suq (bazaar). When he thought it politically expedient in meetings, he could adjust or even reverse his position as deftly as a chameleon altering its color. He never used notes for presentations and always seemed to be able to speak the languages of his clients—English, German, French, Italian, Greek, Arabic, and the Swiss-German dialect.

In later years, Hayek went on to become one of the wealthiest men in the world after he founded the Swatch Group to produce high-style popular watches and the Smart Car Company to make microcompact cars.

The chair that Hayek occupied must have been endowed with the makings for success. It had previously been briefly occupied by Charles Knight, who later went on to become the legendary CEO of the giant Emerson Electric Company. After my first meeting with Knight, I mentioned him to Rita when I returned home from a trip to Zurich, saying, "I met a most impressive young man—twenty-five years old—today who looks and acts like he is already the head of a major corporation. I predict that we will hear more of him in the future."

On my first visit to Hayek Engineering, I was impressed with the firm's versatility. Their engineering contracts ranged from designing a cigarette factory to planning a steel mill.

Hayek exposed me to culture and business practices that, at that time in my career, seemed exotic and worldly. It was as if he was born with genes that included all of the knowledge of his ancient forebears. He thought like a chess player—three steps ahead and with multiple options and ready explanations for every alternative.

The contracts that we handled for the foundry project were for large amounts of money. We had to guard against any kind of gift that might influence our contractor selection decisions. Although it was customary for suppliers to pay for business meals, I picked up the tab for many of them.

After a meeting in Zurich with Hayek, I told him I would be out of touch for a week because Rita and I would soon be on vacation in Switzerland. He said he would do me "the favor" of having his secretary make a hotel reservation for us while we were in Lucerne near his home. When we checked into our room, I gasped when I read the room rate—$50 per night. Our budget called for $10 per night. When I checked out of the hotel and asked for our bill, the clerk said, "Mr. Hayek has paid the bill." For the next two months, I repeatedly called Hayek and asked him to send the hotel bill to me. He continued to stall and finally said, "Your request presents a problem. My company maintains a permanent room in the hotel and the cost is the same to us whether it is occupied or not." Apparently there really was a Santa Claus! I never again let a contractor do me any "favors"—especially one with the guile of a camel merchant.

The Swiss sense of superiority extended to the military. Although Switzerland had not fought a war for centuries, she maintained a strong military force. All males were subject to compulsory military conscription until the age of thirty-two. They kept their uniforms and rifles at the ready in their homes for quick deployment. Swiss soldiers on temporary duty were highly visible in public places.

One of the Swiss Army's traditional duties since the sixteenth century is to provide security for the Pope and the Vatican. The Papal Swiss Guard, with its brilliantly colored and vividly patterned medieval uniforms, cannot be overlooked. But for home duty, the uniforms are similar to those of all other modern armies.

The Swiss believe their fierce military forces kept them out of World War II. But a more logical reason is that the Germans left them alone because they got what they wanted without the necessity of war: secure rail and road access to the battlefields of Italy; the use of Swiss banks for secretly caching loot stolen from millions of murdered Jews and others; and a safe-haven source for highly engineered goods for the German military. During the war, Joseph Göbbels, the German propaganda minister, ridiculed Switzerland's defense claims when he said, "We'll take Switzerland—the little porcupine—sometime on our way back home."

Although our company purchasing agent in Mannheim was a German, he had the negotiating skills of a horse trader. When he squeezed out the last Deutschmark in our favor on contracts, he would then switch to intangible benefits. I once thought he had reached the lowest cost on a contract, but before he would give the final handshake, he insisted that the contractor also agree to buy a John Deere tractor.

I made an effort to learn German by pinning notes with a few new words on my office wall each day. After a few months, I told my secretary to speak only German to me until I bogged down and had to switch back to English. I eventually became fluent enough to discuss routine engineering and administrative subjects in German—especially to those in our office who did not speak English—but if the subject was changed to philosophy, politics, or household matters, I was tongue-tied because of my inadequate vocabulary.

I thought I had reached a new learning plateau when I could pronounce a few mile-long words such as *Gewerbeaufsichtsamt* (Trade Supervisory Office.) The authorities from this office were often at our door to ensure that we complied with the comprehensive industrial rules and regulations on safety, noise, and environmental conditions. Foundries are noisy, smelly, dusty places.

When Mark Twain lived in Heidelberg a century earlier, he wrote of his difficulties in learning to speak long German words. He suggested that it would be easier if the speaker stopped for an intermission and refreshments in the middle of long words and then resumed speaking the word when rested and refreshed.

If Twain could have peered into the future, he would have been amused at the twentieth century writings of George Bailey on the German language. When a lady criticized him for his less-than-perfect pronunciation of some difficult German words, Bailey replied, "Madame, if you want us to speak German together, you must provide the umlauts (a punctuation mark to define the special pronunciation of certain vowels)."

There are various viewpoints on the best European language to use for specific purposes: A Prussian said that German was best for giving "whiplash" sharp military commands. My Berlitz German teacher softly recited a romantic poem to prove that German was soothing to the ear. A king said he spoke Spanish to God, Italian to women, French to men, and German to horses. In the 1960s, German was the best single language to speak while traveling in Central Europe. But English was rapidly overtaking all other languages.

A friend at the John Deere Mannheim factory said, "If I can't get attention and action when I speak German, I switch to English and then I get my way."

Learning German with any fluency late in life is a tough job. Few master it other than a handful of linguistically gifted people—I was not one of them. The accent will seldom be exact and the nuances of words and expressions will seldom be just right. Possibly the worst goof is to incorrectly use words that sound similar but have very different meanings. An American colleague tried to speak college German to our hostess at a party. He thought he told her that her *vorspeisen* (homemade appetizers) were tasty. Instead he said *vorspiel* (sexual foreplay). The hostess and I were only partially successful in keeping straight faces.

It was exhausting to participate in meetings conducted in German. I had to do two demanding things at the same time: thinking about the subject of the meeting while trying to keep up with the language.

The largest and most complex contract for equipment for the new foundry was for the four iron-melting furnaces and their extensive auxiliary equipment. The contractor was located in Düsseldorf in the vast Ruhr industrial district, a two-hour train ride down the Rhine River Valley from Mannheim.

We were surprised that the cities, factories, forges, steel mills, and foundries of the area had been rebuilt so rapidly after the devastation of the war and the stripping of equipment for reparation payments to France and Russia. The Ruhr district with its cartels and large corporations such as Krupp, Thysssen, I.G. Farben, and Vereinigte Stahlwerke provided a large share of the materials and equipment for the Nazi arsenal: coal and coke, chemicals, steel, motor fuels, tanks, and cannons. The sprawling Ruhr district was a constant target for flocks of allied bombers—Vickers Wellingtons, Lancasters, Flying Fortresses, and Liberators. The Western Allies set up a virtual conveyor for dumping bombs on the Ruhr district.

We frequently met in Düsseldorf to oversee the foundry furnace engineering and manufacturing. The train ride from Mannheim on the banks of the Rhine was like a trip through the pages of a classy tourist brochure.

After a visit to the train bar car, it was not hard to fall for the lure of the mythical Siren of Lorelei who allegedly resided atop the misty bluffs of the Rhine River between Koblenz and Bingen, fabled for brooding castles, storybook villages, and surrounding vineyards clinging to hills so steep they were a challenge for mountain goats to climb. Lorelei, an enchanting beauty, combed her blond hair, exposed her beauty, and sang as boats passed below her 160-meter-high rocky perch. Boatmen were allegedly distracted from their navigational duties and killed as their boats crashed onto the treacherous river rocks. The legend of the Siren of Lorelei is the basis for fairytales and songs in most German-speaking countries. It was one of the stories that inspired the Brothers Grimm to gather and publish tales that have delighted children for centuries.

On one of the trips to Düsseldorf with a work companion, I was startled to hear an announcement that we were already at our destination. We ran to our sitting compartment and threw our luggage out the window onto the platform. I knew that the express train would only stop for a couple of minutes. My companion and I jumped from the rapidly accelerating train; I fell, tore my suit, and broke my hand. My companion, who was more agile, maintained his footing. I ignored my fast-swelling hand during an evening of drinking and dining. The next morning our host insisted on an x-ray revealing a compound fracture. I spent the next three days in a hospital and wore a cast for weeks. It was my first involvement with socialized medicine; I found no fault with the experience.

The Germans were reputed to be the best iron and steel industrialists in Europe. Along with their reputation went a number of old traditions: One of them was heavy eating and drinking and hard living. It was almost impossible to avoid our contractor hosts in Düsseldorf meeting us at the train when we arrived the night before our frequent meetings. They insisted on taking us out for late-hour dining, drinking, storytelling, and talking. It was hard to endure the repeated late hours and bad aftertaste the following mornings. I thought I could put a stop to it by refusing to tell them our evening arrival times, but their tradition for hospitality was stronger than our ability to hide our itineraries. Somehow they always found out our schedule and met us at the train station.

When the furnaces were put into operation, the chief engineer for the contractor stood beside the first ladle of molten iron and dramatically made the traditional toast to Saint Barbara—the patron saint for iron and steel making—and concluded it by throwing his felt hat into the 2700 degree Fahrenheit molten metal.

One of the biggest headaches on the foundry project was with the machine that made the molds for the largest iron castings. The heart of the machine was the mold-making unit that was supplied by a US company. The large, expensive machine could not perform at the specified speed even after a company representative came to Mannheim and worked on it for a month. The machine builder claimed it would not perform because John Deere engineers in the US meddled with its design.

The molding machine representative left our office in Mannheim to return to the US under a heavy cloud of recriminations and distrust. As he left the foundry, he walked across a bridge spanning the basement of a bombed-out factory building. An inexperienced Spanish fork truck driver ran into him and pushed him through the bridge railing onto the paving fifteen feet below. He was injured and hospitalized for several weeks. This was the last straw.

It is part of the daily fare on large complex projects to face conflicts and problems with schedules, costs, technical issues, quality, warranties, and errors, but the problem with this machine was off the chart.

A drastic decision was made to junk the expensive machine and replace it with a new one from a German equipment contractor. Replacing the nonperforming American-supplied molding machine with a German machine was embarrassing and costly.

One of the good aspects of dealing with German equipment contractors was their extreme willingness to continue to work with their equipment until it performed satisfactorily and its customers were satisfied. The pride of the engineers and managers was always on the line for their equipment to perform well.

The Mannheim foundry was built across the street from a residential apartment complex. The white masonry wall surrounding the foundry was not enough to contain the noise, dust, and odor emanating during the round-the-clock foundry operating hours. In spite of dust collection systems and noise suppression measures, there were extensive complaints from the apartment occupants about dirt on their clothes hanging out to dry and noise that awakened them at night. The government environment authorities were understanding and cooperative as we took extensive corrective measures. However, the issues with the neighbors were never completely resolved until many decades later when the offending foundry was closed and dismantled.

Although most European locations where we traveled on business were accessible by air, it was usually better to travel via train or to drive. The poor weather of Europe often disrupted air travel schedules. The train systems throughout Germany and Europe were excellent.

German executives often traveled with their secretaries so they could do administrative work while on the road. This custom caused endless speculations on what the "other responsibilities" might be for the secretaries.

Most of our business trips required staying one or two nights in a hotel. I always tried to see the local sights when I had free evenings.

I visited Milan with a colleague to inspect foundry equipment of a type that we were contemplating buying for our Mannheim foundry. While walking past the La Scala Opera House, we were able to buy spur-of-the-moment tickets for an operatic performance. Even though I was not an opera buff, I enjoyed being in such a beautiful and famous hall.

The next day our Milan host drove us past the spot where fascist dictator Benito Mussolini *(il Duce)*, his mistress Clara Patacci, and six others were hung from a wooden beam in 1945. They were hung upside down from meat hooks a few hours after they were ordered from the back of a truck and summarily shot by a group of vengeful Italian partisans. Mussolini's battered body was hung shirtless to dramatize the scorn of his captors and assassins. Patacci's skirt was tied around her legs out of a preposterous concern for her modesty. Mussolini did not achieve the lofty goal he set for himself early in his career: "I shall make my life a masterpiece."

On a December 13 business visit to an industrial city in Sweden to investigate purchasing molten iron holding furnaces, I found that it was Santa Lucia Day, a religious festival honoring Saint Lucia and giving hope for future light after the long, gloomy, northern winter nights. The Santa Lucia festival was already known to me because it was also celebrated in Rock Island, Illinois—my home town—at Augustana College, a school and Lutheran seminary with a strong Swedish heritage. When I took an early morning walk on the cold, snowy streets, I saw young girls in the open-shuttered houses in white dresses with candle crowns on their heads. At lunch and in the evening, candlelit buffets groaned with celebratory food—ginger snaps, pastries, seafood, breads, mulled wine, fruit, and spiced meat balls.

I traveled to a small town in Austria to investigate reports of the unique application of a piece of foundry equipment. When our plane landed, the edge of the runway was lined with a dozen curious white storks. It was the first time I ever saw the stately four-foot-tall birds.

I learned from my Austrian host about the country's famous capacity for courtesy and diplomacy. I spoke to him in my best bad German. After some time passed, he said, "Although speaking to you in German is fine with me, perhaps you would be more comfortable speaking another language. I speak seven, but unfortunately English is not one of them." We struggled on in German.

From the beginning, there were uneasy undercurrents from both sides of the Atlantic on how to design and build foundries. The proud Germans had long experience in the iron business and the John Deere Americans also had an extensive history of building foundries; each was insistent in "doing it our way."

In the beginning, the US side usually prevailed because it controlled the purse strings. But as time passed and after significant company management changes were made in the US and in Germany, we started to evaluate the merits of engineering with less regard for the origin of the ideas. The later phases of the foundry-building project proceeded with fewer conflicts.

The Mannheim foundry had to satisfy many customers. It had to please iron casting users in the Mannheim tractor factory as well as those in other company factories in Germany, France, and Spain. The new John Deere diesel engine factory in Orleans, France was the most demanding customer with its need for complex, precision engine castings. The Mannheim foundry management team, assisted by many visiting US specialists, struggled for a long time until it could deliver quality iron castings.

On a warm summer day, a Mannheim factory official took Bill Hewitt, John Deere's CEO, on a tour of the foundry. At the end of the tour, he brought him to my office for several minutes of discussion. As he left he said, "I don't want you to make this foundry your lifetime work."

I thought his remark was slightly harsh, but that it probably was just his way of bantering. The factory official came back the next day and said, "Bill Hewitt asked me to tell you his remark was not meant to be critical of your work here." At the time, I did not fully realize the pressure on Hewitt because of the company's European marketing difficulties and heavy financial loses.

The Mannheim foundry superintendent had difficulty with the challenges of managing the new foundry. The foundry customers were dissatisfied with the casting quality and delivery reliability. A new, highly experienced and competent manager from another company was hired to succeed him. He brought in a demanding, "tree shaking" management style. He soon improved the foundry operation and went on to successfully manage it for decades.

After three years of managing the engineering, construction, and start-up of the new foundry, we closed our Mannheim office. The foundry project was completed on schedule and within the budgeted cost. The long-term remaining issues as well as other newly developing foundry projects were turned over to the foundry operating group. Our staff was reassigned except for an engineer and a secretary who resigned. Most of them went on to long successful careers within the company—some in higher positions. Several said, "The finest time of my career was while I worked in the demanding, team-like environment of the Mannheim foundry construction office."

The Mannheim foundry operated for many years as an integral part of John Deere's European manufacturing strategy.

Years later after I retired from John Deere, I considered my role in building the Mannheim foundry to be one of my most rewarding and satisfying professional experiences. I expanded my knowledge of engineering and manufacturing, but more important, I learned about human nature, diplomacy, and give and take at negotiating tables. Engineering, based in technical facts and immutable principles, was much easier to master than human issues.

For the next year, I worked in the John Deere regional headquarters in Heidelberg. I worked on projects that were underway to retool factories in Germany and Spain, to start up a new factory in France, and to provide oversight for new foundry projects in Mannheim.

Working in the the Heidlberg office gave me a fine opportunity to see how the many facets of the company needed to work harmoniously together for success.

During this time, a veteran senior company officer and board member moved to Heidelberg to head up John Deere's business in Europe, Africa, and Middle East. Until then the management structure was fragmented. All divisions—marketing, manufacturing, engineering, and finance—now reported to the new managing director.

I once read a military history book where an authoritative and decisive army colonel was described as a "gravel crunching" colonel. The new John Deere managing director was a "gravel crunching" executive.

He could also be kind and understanding. I had several meetings with him where he could have chastised me for my inexperienced responses to his questions. He kindly helped me through the meetings.

Although he confidently and decisively took charge of the activities of the regional office, it would take more than a decade of relentless, grinding work and several false starts (futile pursuit of joint ventures with other companies) until straightforward, relentless slogging led to profitability and solid success for John Deere in Europe.

Iron Casting

Cast Iron Engine Block

CHAPTER 8

THE LUDWIG ERHARD ERA
1963 TO 1968

Of a truth the gods do not give the same man everything: you know how to gain a victory, Hannibal, but you do not know how to make use of it.
—Livy's History of Rome

Ludwig Erhard

In early 1963—at the time I started traveling to Germany—Konrad Adenauer was politically squeezed to relinquish his more than a decade-long role as chancellor of West Germany. Ludwig Erhard was elected as the second postwar chancellor. In the US, John Kennedy had just been assassinated and Lyndon Johnson was the new occupant of the White House. Erhard would serve as chancellor from 1964 to 1968.

Dr. Erhard was an economist, teacher, writer, finance minister, and World War I artillery veteran who was severely wounded in Ypres, Belgium. He was a brilliant, confident, and decisive economic policy wonk.

Like Adenauer, Erhard stayed clear of the Nazis during the war. He spent the war years working on his favorite subject—the study of economics. He developed his ideas on what would be necessary to restore the economic health of postwar Germany based on free markets, free trade, and a stable currency, with the government playing the role of a strong referee. For the rest of his life, these ideas would be his bedrock.

Erhard was difficult to pigeonhole. Although he was aware of and understood politics, he was not a politician. He thought he was good at balancing his knowledge of hardheaded economic theories with his practical experience and understanding of human and social values.

He believed he was well-suited to explain his economic theories to the German people. He thought if they followed his theories and were treated well by their government, they would improve their lives, respect each other, and live responsibly.

He often said economic growth would solve problems better than labor unions and government rules. He explained, "It is easier to give everyone a bigger piece from an ever-growing cake than to struggle over dividing up a small cake."

Erhard opposed "co-determination" (labor and management sitting together on supervisory boards of directors) of larger corporations, one of the most cherished beliefs of the labor lobby. He thought only owners, not employees, could make proper entrepreneurial decisions based on risk and reward assessments.

Erhard also opposed any moves toward a united Europe with integrated fiscal and economic policies administrated by a central bureaucracy. His views put him in constant conflict with powerful pro-united Europe forces.

Erhard started to become politically prominent in 1947 when he was selected by the Americans and British to chair the newly created Special Office for Credit and Money. His free market ideas immediately put him into conflict with socialist-oriented government officials who were obsessed with income equality and high taxes for the wealthy. Erhard said it was better to let the wealthy keep their money to invest in industry and recovery from the war than to tax it away for dubious uses by government bureaucrats.

He had a dim view of government bureaucracies. He said, "Every planned economy rests on the assumption that some bureaucracy with mountains of available data can be wiser than the consumers who they serve. This is complete economic nonsense."

After the war, Erhard recognized the obligation for Germany to pay war reparations to the allied victors, but he did not think it made sense to do it with industrial equipment taken from Germany. He thought the machinery should be kept to produce goods that could be sold for cash; the cash could then be used for paying reparations. This was in direct conflict with the Russians and French, who carted away everything possible in their occupied territories leaving factories, transportation systems, power generation stations, and offices picked as clean as animal carcasses after being dined on by hungry wolf packs.

In 1949 stiff-necked Adenauer appointed jovial Erhard to be his economics minister even though he disliked him. Everything about Erhard's personal life irked Adenauer: his sloppy dress; constant cigar chomping and smoking; beer drinking; interest in fast cars; overeating (he was nicknamed *Der Dicke* –The Fat One); card playing; listening to Mozart operas with his wife rather than studying government documents; devotion to sports; congenial optimism; faith in the goodness of most people; and refusal to engage in political treachery. Erhard liked to study the big issues at the expense of staying on top of the details for managing the government. All of these things outraged the studious, ascetic Adenauer and were in sharp contrast to his values: hard work, modest personal habits, distrust of human nature, micromanaging, manipulation of people, and rigid adherence to strict Christian principles.

Immediately after Erhard became Adenaur's economics minister, their relationship deteriorated further because Erhard rigidly stuck to his rational and proven ideas on the economy whereas the ever-pragmatic Adenauer bent in the direction of the prevailing political winds.

With the outbreak of the Korean War in 1950, the demand for German goods shot up. Panic hoarding of goods and food occurred because of public fear that the events in Korea could lead to a Russian invasion of Western Europe. Production rose dramatically and unemployment fell.

The Korean War raised the worry flags in Europe and America. Stalin egged on North Korea to invade South Korea. Many drew the conclusion that this was a diversionary tactic and a prelude for Russia to take military action in Europe.

The occupying Americans still called the shots in West Germany through the office of High Commissioner John McCloy. His staff insisted that planning and controls would solve the economic problems in West Germany caused by the Korean War. Erhard aired an opposite viewpoint in a newspaper article, "Only primitive minds could still suggest that the solution to the current problem could be found in more planning."

By 1955 the highly-touted "economic miracle" in West Germany was evident and credit was usually given to Erhard. But he said, "It was no miracle; it was the logical result of policies that were carefully considered in advance."

When the European Common Market was established in 1957, Minister of Economics Erhard reluctantly supported it to back the political desires of Chancellor Adenauer.

Later in 1957—largely by shamelessly taking credit for Erhard's economic theories for West German prosperity—Adenauer won a stunning political victory when he was reelected chancellor. He still despised Erhard, but he had to continue to tolerate him as his economic minister.

The growth of the West German economy was explosive; it continued to skyrocket throughout the 1950s. The available labor pool—even after absorbing millions of refugee workers from the east—was exhausted. The borders were opened to a controlled flood of "guest workers" from other countries with high unemployment.

My personal observations in our Heidelberg neighborhood and when we traveled supported the often-reported stories that the economic miracle extended to all citizens. People appeared to be well clothed and fed. Many owned cars—although modest in size and luxury—and housing appeared to be adequate. The entire country seemed to pulse with steadily growing prosperity. I never saw a beggar on the streets. The election promise of Herbert Hoover and the Republicans in the US from thirty-five years earlier was approaching realization in West Germany: A chicken in every pot and a car in every garage.

This, only a couple of decades after the entire demoralized country lay wasted with a smashed economy; a starving, ill-clothed, and poorly housed population; a large percent of her male population dead or in Russian prisons; dysfunctional transportation, communications, and power supply systems; nearly worthless currency; and a government.in chaos. But much of the talent and organization that supplied the mighty Nazi arsenals was still intact and when it was allowed to again shift into high gear, economic recovery was swift in West Germany—but not so in East Germany.

By the late 1950s Erhard's physical and mental energy diminished. He was drained by Adenauer's never-ending defamation to ensure that he did not become his successor as chancellor.

During Erhard's time as chancellor, he was criticized for not being courageous and aggressive. He agreed with his detractors when he responded, "That's the way it is. I have the courage of a dove; I lack the gall."

Erhard tried to introduce a relaxed and collegial atmosphere into the government with a minimum of top-down orders. His staff, which was used to its orders coming from above, performed like an orchestra with an absent conductor.

He made a serious blunder by declining the top chair of his political party even though as chancellor it could have been his. He foolishly and naively left it to ex-chancellor Adenauer, who used it as forum for viciously opposing Erhard's will.

In dealings between Adenauer and Erhard, ever-crafty Adenauer always danced a step ahead in strategic thinking, was always cocksure of his position, and usually—but not always—got his way.

In 1965, West Germany held a parliamentary election. The middle class people, to whom Erhard had appealed for most of his political life, remembered his economic leadership—even though most of them did not understand his theories—in rebuilding the war-ravaged West German economy. They gave him a substantial reelection victory while Adenauer continued to lob negative jibes from the sidelines.

Late in 1965, Chancellor Erhard visited Washington well prepared to discuss an agenda of issues of mutual interest with President Johnson; Johnson was not inclined to listen because of his preoccupation with problems in Vietnam. Johnson took Erhard into a small room and for fifteen minutes treated him like a Texas cotton field overseer might treat his field hands in an earlier generation as he crudely demanded physical and financial contributions from Germany for the Vietnam War. Erhard, who was stunned at Johnson's crude, bullying demands, refused to submit to his trademark, overbearing method of "persuasion." Johnson's advisors who were present were embarrassed and shocked at such boorishness.

If Johnson had read about some of Erhard's confrontations soon after the war with the occupying US forces, he would have known he could be a tough nut to crack when important issues were at stake. In 1948 Erhard, on his own initiative and contrary to US wishes, abolished food rationing and price controls in West Germany. General Lucius Clay, the military commander of the Western Allies in Germany, said, "Herr Erhard, my advisors tell me you have relaxed the rationing system. That is a mistake when there is such a food scarcity."

Erhard said, "*Herr General*, I did not relax it; I abolished it. It will now work better with a free market since we have established the new stable Deutschmark to replace the inefficient black market economy." The old currency, the Reichsmark, was often called "wallpaper marks" because it was so distrusted and inflation was so rampant.that people did much of their trading on the black market with cigarettes, batteries, tires, potatoes, shoes, stockings, and coal. Desperate woman sometimes even traded themselves for urgently needed necessities. Some products were priced in cigarettes—six hundred cigarettes would buy a bicycle. Erhard's economic policies and actions were like a steroid shot to the West German economy.

While he was chancellor, Erhard's principle achievements were reducing German dependence on the US and establishing diplomatic ties with Israel.

Whereas Erhard's elevation to the chancellor's office was well deserved, his long standing lack of political and foreign affairs skills and interests and his resistance to the entrenched public concepts of socialism doomed him to a short and ineffective reign. He also became increasingly out of step with the youth of the country, who regarded World War II as something out of dusty history books and who took the country's prosperity for granted.

In late 1966 Erhard seemed to have lost his touch and his physical vigor declined further; he was becoming an anachronism. When his supporters abandoned him, he quietly and honorably resigned. He lived ten more years while continuing to serve as a member of the West German parliament.

The quotation noted at the beginning of this chapter from Livy's *History of Rome* (Of a truth the gods do not give the same man everything: you know how to gain a victory, Hannibal, but you do not know how to make use of it) could aptly apply to Erhard. His crowning achievement was brilliantly conceiving and implementing the West German postwar economic policies; his weakness was not firmly grasping the reigns of the federal government when they were handed to him.

With the resignation of the mild-mannered and ever-optimistic Erhard, the nation abandoned many of his sound economic theories and moved toward an expanding, costly welfare state with little concern for how it would be funded. Most of the public and the politicians understood that the economic discipline and restraints advocated by Erhard were good for them, but they opted for the pleasure of wine and easy living even though they knew there would be a bill that must be paid later. George Bernard Shaw explained the situation well when he said, "A government with the policy to rob Peter to pay Paul can be assured of the support of Paul."

In December 1966, Erhard was succeeded as chancellor by Kurt Georg Kiesinger, a lawyer and expert on foreign affairs who governed during my last year of living in Germany. He was a former Nazi, a fact that clouded his time in office. During much of his term, he focused on reducing tensions with the blustering Soviet Bloc countries.

Considering Chancellor Kiesinger's two history-defining predecessors during the tumultuous postwar era in West Germany, he received the same amount of attention as a person would if he spoke at an aeronautical conference following Wilbur and Orville Wright.

THE LUDWIG ERHARD ERA

President Johnson and Chancellor Erhard
Washington, DC

US High Commissioner McCloy
and German Chancellor Erhard

CHAPTER 9

THE LOOMING BEAR TO THE EAST

I cannot forecast to you the action of Russia. It is a riddle, wrapped in a mystery, inside an enigma; but perhaps there is a key. That key is Russian national interest.
—Winston Churchill

And so it was necessary to teach people not to think and make judgments, to compel them to see the non-existent, and argue the opposite of what was obvious to everyone.
—Boris Pasternak

The tactics used by the East European Communist parties after the war to eliminate their rivals and gain unchallenged power did not seem at all unusual. Political life was already imbued with violence.
—Jan Gross (Polish writer)

Whoever occupies a territory also imposes on it his own social system. Everyone imposes his own system as far as his army has power to do so.
—Joseph Stalin

Facts no longer made contact with the theory (of communism), which had risen above the facts on clouds of nonsense, rather like a theological system. The point was not to believe the theory, but to repeat it ritualistically and in such a way that both belief and doubt become irrelevant. In this way the concept of truth disappeared from the intellectual landscape, and was replaced by that of power.
—George Orwell

The Russian Bear to the East
(Stalin in Disguise)

When the alliance between Russia and the Western Allied Forces withered immediately after World War II (in Russia it was called "The Great Patriotic War"), it became evident that profound and irreconcilable political and cultural differences existed between the communist and the democratic worlds. Winston Churchill dramatically defined the differences with an often-quoted line from his speech given in Fulton, Missouri in 1946: "From Stettin on the Baltic to Trieste on the Adriatic, an iron curtain has descended across the continent." "Iron curtain" instantly became the chosen phrase to describe anything to do with communism. "Cold War" soon followed as the term for defining the conditions that would prevail in the East and the West for five more decades.

It was hard for the West to understand the Russian mindset. To the communist leaders, the supremacy of communism made it the only logical system for governing. They believed it was scientifically superior to all others and would outpace the capitalistic West. They believed when communism was fully proven and accepted in Russia and Eastern Europe, it would inevitably spread to Western Europe and then to the rest of the world. The Russians thought although Soviet-style communism would lead to a worldwide transformation, it would need to be expedited with persuasion by the security police. Their persuasion methods rivaled those of the Mafia as they convinced their victims to climb into car trunks when encouraged with ice picks and hot soldering irons.

Ordinary people did not give a fig for high-blown theories of government. They only wanted adequate food, respectable clothing and housing, decent social services, education, cars, vacations, personal comfort, and rewarding jobs. They wanted high-quality material possessions and services that would improve their dreary lives.

The communist economic system focused on designing and manufacturing military and industrial equipment; it gave short shrift to consumer goods and services. The Russian authorities assigned to manage the limited part of the economy dedicated to consumer goods never could get the hang of making quality products, efficiently growing food, distributing goods, supplying repair parts and services, providing entertainment free of propaganda, and listening to the voice of the market. Consumer goods were shoddy; half the food produced spoiled and rotted before it got to dining tables; consumers wasted countless hours searching for food and necessities; and people starved in a country that for centuries had been the bread basket of Europe.

A British politician's taunting remark about his opponent could be modified and applied to Russia: "We live on an island made of coal surrounded by an ocean teeming with fish. Yet with the economic policies and political leadership of my opponent, we are cold and hungry." The resources and opportunities in Russia were without limit and yet they remained inaccessible to ordinary citizens.

The fact that communism fundamentally failed to work was blamed by the Russians on poor training, poor administration, inadequate discipline, and unreasonable resistance by the decadent West. In Russia and her controlled territories, the theory of communism won out over capitalism only when stuffed down the throats of the hapless citizens by overpowering security police. If harsh persuasion methods for converting people to Russian communism did not work, there was the "next level" such as the annihilation of the prosperous Cossack farmers in southern Russia and the Ukraine; the mass murder of all military officers and intelligentsia in Poland; and the never-ending pogroms against Russian Jews.

Russia also thought she should insulate her people from any exposure to the Western world for fear they would be seduced by the lure of its superficial façade. After World War I, a whimsical song expressed a similar concern with rustic American soldiers when they returned home from France:

> How ya gonna keep 'em down on the farm
> After they've seen Paree

But there was nothing whimsical with Russian soldiers and civilians who had seen the West during the war and contrasted it to their threadbare motherland and the absurd political hooey spouted by their leaders. Many rioted when they were rounded up for forcible return to their harsh homeland; some even committed suicide. They knew when they returned home, their fate likely would be a death sentence, summary execution, severe punishment, or shipment to Siberia to be abused and worked to death. They could not be allowed to contaminate others with their tales of a better life in the West in countries with free and democratic governments.

When Russian troops came into western European territories and contrasted the household goods, fine buildings, and well-stocked stores with their crude household utensils and furniture, hovels for homes, and stores stocked only with rudimentary goods, they learned that the Russian economic system was inferior and their government was deceitful.

The Russians flaunted their military might and the claimed superiority of communism with endless processions staged in Moscow's Red Square. The parades were made up of tanks, rockets, trucks with gaudy whitewall tires, artillery, goose-stepping troops, and posters exalting their political leaders. Overhead, the latest model aircraft streaked by. Watching over the spectacle from the ancient stone Kremlin towers were the expressionless old men—some drooling—who sat on the Politburo and mannequin-like senior military officers. The whole lot looked like they could be models for popular wooden nesting dolls. The annual Red Square pageant was rehearsed endlessly; it was done with the precision of a Rockette show in Manhattan's Radio City Music Hall but with less entertainment value. And no hint of what people really cared about—quality food, clothing, and housing.

Major agreements regarding post-World War II Europe were made in conferences held in Tehran, Iran in 1943 and in Yalta, Russia in early 1945. Leaders of the "Big Three"—Roosevelt, Churchill, and Stalin—attended.

After the war, in late 1945, a third "Big Three" conference was held in Potsdam, Germany. This time the representatives were Truman (replacing deceased Roosevelt), Atlee (just voted into the Prime Minister's office in Great Britain) and Stalin. Some of the best-remembered and most painful decisions—made in secrecy—were the cavalier forced repatriation of millions of ethnic Germans and the arbitrary remapping of much of Eastern Europe.

But good and necessary agreements were also made at the "Big Three" conferences: Russia was to enter the war against Japan after Germany's defeat; free elections were to be held in Eastern European countries (this would never happen); defeated Germany was to be demilitarized; and the United Nations was to be established.

At a cocktail party that I attended while living in Heidelberg, a guest fumed about Russians being allowed to hold sway over East Germany and the countries of Eastern Europe. An informed student of recent history reminded him of the three secret meetings—especially the Yalta meeting—of the Allied Powers. At those meetings, the die was cast for much of Europe with callous nonchalance. The fate of Europe would be determined by the locations of the occupying armed forces—Russian and the Western Allied Forces—at the time hostilities with Germany ended. Communism and control would prevail in the East and capitalism and freedom in the West. Stalin insisted that he needed control of the Eastern European countries as a buffer zone to protect Russia from future invasions from the West. When the eastern countries learned the results of the secret "Big Three" conferences, they believed they had been betrayed by Roosevelt, whose boundless idealism combined with his naiveté, proved no match for Stalin's cynical use of raw power with total disregard for freedom and human rights. Throughout Eastern Europe, Yalta became the byword for betrayal.

Roosevelt and most Americans thought Stalin was capable of sitting at a conference table and mutually working out reasonable and honorable decisions. They did not understand that he was partly a rational, Europeanized Peter the Great looking to the West and partly an autocratic, Asian Genghis Khan, the leader of the Golden Horde that ruthlessly conquered most of Eurasia 500 years before the Age of Enlightenment. Fyodor Dostoyevsky, a Russian writer and thinker, said, "In Europe we are Asiatic, whereas in Asia we are European."

Roosevelt did not trust many people, and he was normally a superior judge of character, but he misjudged Stalin. Some say he did not stand up to Stalin's bluster and demands because he was exhausted and gravely ill. In photos at the Yalta conference, he looks like he already had one foot over the threshold into the next world. He would die two months later.

Others asked what more he could have done short of starting a war with Russia's battle-toughened Red Army to try to push it out of the areas it had won and occupied after years of frightful battles. Stalin thought the Russians had carried a disproportionate burden in the war and deserved a large reward for the loss of ten percent of his country's population—fourteen million military deaths and seven million civilian. Many additional millions of Russians died before and during the war, but those by the hand of Stalin when he did not think they enthusiastically supported the war and his system of government or simply at his whim.

The inequality in the level of prosperity between Russia and the West, as well as the vast historical, political, and cultural differences, made it virtually impossible for there to be a basis for common thinking; most people on either side simply could not comprehend the other.

The Russian leaders could not believe or accept that their totalitarian system of communism was fundamentally flawed and unworkable; to force most people to freely accept communism was like trying to jam a metric nut on a British bolt. When Stalin was asked how he could continue to promote the Marxist-Leninist theories of communism in the face of evidence that it wasn't working, he responded as though he lived in never-never land. He allegedly replied, "If the facts do not support the theories, then I adjust the facts." Stalin was a master of "reality distortion" when he temporarily disengaged his tether from reality and objectivity.

Russian leaders were willing to pay a sky-high price of human lives for the introduction and establishment of communism. Stalin callously commented on lost lives: A single death is a tragedy; a million is a statistic. The Russians were willing to pay any price to introduce the "goodness of communism" and eliminate the "evils of capitalism." Stalin's cynical words recall a similar line written a century earlier by Fyodor Dostoyevsky: However much you tinker with the world, you can't make it very easy to control, but by cutting off a hundred million heads there is no more resistance and the job is a cinch.

In contrast, Winston Churchill summed up the mindset of most of the Western world about the best way to govern, "It has been said that democracy is the worst form for government except for all others that have been tried."

In the postwar years in Europe, the West was led by the US and her NATO allies and the East by the Soviet Union and the Warsaw Pact members. For decades following the war, the media was saturated with news of East-West posturing, espionage, propaganda, arms races, threats, sports competitions, proxy wars, suspicion, distrust, and blustering. The line between the East and West was razor sharp.

The military threat to the West became much more worrisome when Russia set off her first atomic bomb in 1949. This was followed by a hydrogen bomb in 1955. With nuclear weapons no longer a monopoly of the US, the world military balance required a major strategic adjustment.

While we lived in Heidelberg in the 1960s, we were surrounded by the massive presence of the resident US military. When tensions were high during periodic cycles of Russian threats, we had a fanciful vision of our highly torqued and motivated soldiers and airmen perpetually girded, loaded for bear, and ready to sprint to their waiting tanks, planes, and jeeps to race east to face the invading Red Army. This vision made us feel safe—but also a bit nervous.

We often heard our military friends speak of the possibility of the Russians invading West Germany through the Fulda Gap, a large flat area northeast of Frankfurt that was ideal for large scale infantry and tank maneuvering. Pessimists imagined the Red Army to be as limitless and unstoppable as Genghis Kahn's marauding Mongolian horde that swept into Europe from the east in the thirteen century. It was scarcely more than an hour drive from our home to the Fulda Gap; it was scary.

In spite of the closeness of the Red Army to where we lived in Heidelberg, I never saw a Russian or Eastern Bloc soldier. Cross-border travel was under close control and communist currencies were virtually valueless in the West.

Both sides—with their nuclear weapons—were held in tight check. The East and the West were like a pair of scorpions warily circling before the start of a death dance knowing the lethal outcome for both of them if they embraced. However, there was always a gnawing concern in our minds that a vodka-soaked Russian soldier or a disgruntled American GI might open Pandora's box and accidentally trigger a nuclear military exchange with appalling consequences. Although it seemed that nuclear weapons guaranteed there would never be a deliberate hot war between Russia and the US, it would be hard to keep the weapons holstered in the event of an unintended military incident. The inevitable Armageddon following the use of nuclear weapons was unimaginable. From the vantage point of a half century later, it is now clear that the US and Russia both played from the same rule book on one point—when pushed to the brink of war, they would both ease off just before lethal contact was made. But in the 1960s, the Armageddon scenario was plausible.

Any doubts about the potential horrors of nuclear power were dispelled decades later at the time of the Chernobyl atomic power plant catastrophe in Russia (30,000 people were doomed for slow radiation death) and the similar Fukushima Daiichi disaster in Japan. Many lives were lost and enormous areas of land and water became toxic when these atomic power plants massively failed.

After the merciless 1956 bludgeoning of the Hungarians by the Russians during the Budapest uprising, the Chinese abandonment of her alliance with Russia, the "trashing" of all of the economies touched by Russia, and the spread of corruption in Russia, the entire communist house of cards started to fray and wobble. Nevertheless, it would continue to exist for decades under the harsh, twisting heel of the Russian enforcers.

For years the Cold War diverted the wealth and strength of the US and NATO nations and Russian and Warsaw Pact countries from peaceful endeavors; nevertheless the adversaries maintained a balance that kept the world from another war of the scope of World War II.

Early in World War II, it seemed that the Russian bear was only a bumbling cub. The Germans, in a massive Blitzkrieg attack, confidently and successfully invaded Russia in June of 1941. At first they bested the Russians in every way and at every turn. But the Germans could not overcome the frigid winters; the never-ending expanses of land; and eventually the dogged determination and bravery of the developing Red Army. The invasion bogged down and extended into the bitter, ruthless winter; it became a disaster for Germany and ended her acclaimed invincibility.

After Russia's initial successes in stopping the Nazi invasion and then counterattacking, it slowly became obvious that her popular symbol, the bear, was an apt representation for her people—ferocious, cunning, tenacious, merciless, unpredictable, and able to absorb unlimited punishment and hardships. When German soldiers were ordered to the Eastern Front, they considered it their death sentence. Hitler arrogantly and stupidly disregarded the deadly fate of Napoleon's army when it similarly failed to capture Moscow during a numbing Russian winter military campaign.

One of the bloodiest conflicts of the war on the Eastern Front and a major turning point was the Battle of Stalingrad with General Friedrich von Paulus leading his 300,000-strong German 6th Army. His poorly supplied and inadequately clothed army became frozen, broken down, diseased, hungry, wounded, dysfunctional, and dispirited during its ill-timed winter attack on Stalingrad. When von Paulus thought it could get no worse, his army was annihilated by the unforgiving, winter-hardened Russian Red Army led by General Zhukov and others. Only a handful of von Paulus' captured soldiers ever returned home after years of brutal forced labor in Siberian work camps.

From a distant vantage point, one could imagine the Battle for Stalingrad as the methodical working of a giant, crushing pendulum that swung east—under German control—to its maximum limit of motion at Stalingrad. And after a pause to regain strength, it swung back—this time under Russian control—to its point of origin in Germany. The utter desolation and death in the path of the pendulum, as it swung both ways, was so vast it would sicken a vulture.

The few mauled Germans who survived the Russian battles stumbled back home from their ill-fated venture through the battlefield wreckage and ravaged land left from their earlier invasion. The proud, arrogant hounds of hell that confidently swept into much of western Russia departed like whipped, whimpering curs. It was the beginning of the end for the humbled Nazi Army.

After Stalingrad, the German people slowly began to realize they had been pumped full of hooey by the Nazi propaganda machine and that the outcome of the war—especially from the relentless and merciless Red Army—would be unthinkably bad for them. They cringed at the thought of the terrible revenge they sensed was coming to settle accounts for the Nazi army's atrocious behavior in Russia. They disregarded their government's propaganda about forthcoming super-weapons and imminent victory; they recognized they were going to be shellacked again for the second time in a quarter century.

Overlaying the invasion of Russia was the utter Nazi contempt for Slavic people. The Nazis thought Slavs were scarcely better than animals suitable for slaughter, starvation, enslavement, and extermination. They planned to use the vast conquered land of Russia for *Lebensraum* (living space), a source of raw materials, and for slave labor.

The barbaric behavior of the Nazis, with their superior attitude, when they first poured into Russia made it easier for the victorious Red Army to reciprocate in the same manner when they would later—with their churning tanks, pulverizing artillery, and relentless infantry—grind across Germany to Berlin.

Revenge became the policy of Russia when she invaded Germany. A Russian general reminded his commanders of their "holy oath to avenge themselves against the enemy for all of the atrocities committed on Soviet soil" and their "responsibility to repay the Germans for their evil." The grim Russian policy was carried out with eagerness and efficiency. Strict communist theoreticians claimed the Germans also "deserved retribution" because they practiced capitalism. Mao Zedong of China had a similar viewpoint: The death of one worker weighs heavily like a mountain, while that of a bourgeois (capitalist) as light as a feather.

I raptly listened to the stories of my German colleagues who had been soldiers on the Eastern Front and were among the few who returned home. Their bearing was like prisoners who had miraculously received eleventh hour reprieves from death row. Their pitiful stories of the thousands of their comrades who perished and were unceremoniously dumped into frigid graves could hardly be imagined.

After the war ended, the triumphant Russians thought they had carried the heaviest load in defeating the Nazis and deserved a large percent of the booty. The victorious Red Army was still intact, and by 1951 they had the atomic bomb. They believed they had the right and the strength to do exactly as they desired in what became East Germany, and they were supremely confident that communism would bury capitalism because of its inherent superiority. It was a heady time for the Russians.

The fear of the Russian bear going on a rampage to the West was palpable. The general feeling was that if she decided to move outside her normal sphere of influence in Russia and the Eastern Bloc countries, she would likely first invade West Germany and probably precipitate World War III. The Germans were especially fearful their country would be the target for the wide scale use of atomic bombs that would annihilate their population and leave their cities and farms a toxic wasteland for an indefinite time.

The fear was not without basis. The cold war—built on distrust, suspicion, and misunderstanding—was at a high point. In 1962, war with the US over establishing Russian nuclear missile bases in Cuba was narrowly averted. Since the end of World War II, Russia had repeatedly demonstrated that she would swing her lethal claws and snap her sharp teeth when irritated or challenged. Restive Hungary, East Germany, and Czechoslovakia were slapped down hard when they tried to shake off the bear's unwelcome and suffocating embrace.

In 1964, the mysterious and sinister Russian politburo deposed bombastic Nikita Khrushchev and replaced him with *apparatchik* (bureaucrat) Leonid Brezhnev. It was unknown what went on in the Byzantine halls of the Kremlin as the people of Russia and the rest of the world waited for the "red smoke" announcing Khrushchev's successor; it was a scary time and cause for great anxiety. When most people thought of the Kremlin, it brought to their minds Rasputin (the Czar's "witch doctor") and Ivan the Terrible. West Germans in particular wondered what mischief newly elected Brezhnev planned for them.

When Russian leadership changed there could be total and surprising reversals. Everyone remembered Khrushchev's stunning denunciation of godlike Stalin for his mass executions of his opponents based on trumped up charges; foreign policy blunders; failure of the brutal and terrorizing collectivization of agriculture; appalling loss of lives in World War II; and allowing Germany to invade vast areas of Russia early in the war. And they remembered that Stalin had summarily executed most of his senior military officers early in the war because he did not trust them.

Russia needed a scary boogeyman to control her population. Tony Judt, an historian ripe with knowledge of postwar history, explained: "The communist state was in a permanent condition of undeclared war against her own citizens. Like Lenin, her leaders understood the need for enemies; they were constantly mobilizing against their foes—most importantly their domestic foes."

The entire Russian Empire was plagued with economic stagnation, rampant corruption, and inefficiency.

A broadly read and slightly eccentric social acquaintance who lived in Heidelberg was given to drawing on ancient lore—particularly when his imagination was stimulated by wine—and projecting it forward into modern circumstances. At a social gathering, he compared the modern Russian Red Army to the Red Death featured in Edgar Allen Poe's mid-nineteenth century story "The Masque of the Red Death." He first reminded us of the story's plot:

> Prince Prospero, a medieval nobleman, and his friends dined, danced, and reveled at a masked ball in the seeming isolation and security of his remote mountain castle thinking they could safely wait out an approaching epidemic of the deadly Red Death (bubonic plague) that was devastating the surrounding country.
>
> In spite of Prince Prospero's diligent precautions, at the last chime of midnight, a mysterious, uninvited guest appeared in his Gothic castle halls among the waltzing, swirling revelers as they danced to the pulsating, other-worldly Gypsy music. The prince was horrified to find a strange, ghostly visitor among the dancers. He was hooded and cloaked in blood-red velvet. The vivid red pustules on his face and his burning breath confirmed that he was the bearer of the hideous and fatal bubonic pestilence.

My imaginative friend poured another glass of red wine and mused about West Germany living in the ominous shadow of the looming Red Army, asking:

> Was the West any safer from the threatening Red Army than Prospero was from the intrusion of the fatal Red Death? Would Brezhnev send his army into West Germany as an uninvited guest and if it came, would it bring the Soviet version of the dreaded

Red Death—the death of democracy, the suppression of human rights and freedom, and the annihilation of the thriving economy? And even worse, would the coming of the dreaded Red Army open Pandora's box, releasing atomic weapons, and initiating the biblical battle of Armageddon that ends life on earth?

My friend's imaginative metaphor was clever and amusing but unsettling. It necessitated ordering another bottle of red wine to calm our jittery minds.

Having the Red Army as our next door neighbor made us feel as anxious as nesting chickens beside a cage of red foxes.

Although we enjoyed traveling, we never visited Russia or Eastern Bloc countries while we lived in Europe because of the burden and nuisance of securing visas. The communist officials suppressed contacts with the west as if it would put its citizens in league with the devil.

At a later time, after the fall of communism, I visited a drab Hungarian border town directly across from vibrant, sparkling Austria. I stopped in a once-fashionable restaurant for afternoon tea. It looked like the clock stopped in the 1930s: tired art deco style; floors covered with worn out linoleum; and dreary, tattered furniture. The plain wooden shelves of an adjacent grocery store offered dumpy, basic products packaged in drab boxes, bottles, and bags. The decrepit, ill-maintained building facades in the neighborhood looked like theater stage settings resurrected from an ancient storage warehouse. It confirmed that I had not missed much by not previously traveling to places sullied by the communist economic and political system.

Instead of building a consumer goods society to benefit her citizens, Russia poured money, manpower, and technology into her formidable military and security capability. She could not do otherwise; if she let up on her army and iron-fisted security apparatus, citizens certainly would revolt. Russia had few qualms about using her armed might when she thought she could get away with it. And she did get away with it in the Eastern Bloc countries that resisted her. Western European countries and most Americans were also wary of the restive and unpredictable Russian bear.

While we lived in West Germany, we probably need not have feared the Russians, but we did not know it until decades later. Tony Judt wrote this in the early 2005:

> The illusion seemed plausible that communism was reformable; that Stalinism had taken a wrong turn, a mistake that could

still be corrected; and that the core ideals of democratic pluralism (coexistence of multiple groups) might somehow still be compatible with the structures of Marxist collectivism. That illusion was crushed under tank treads during the Russian and Warsaw Pact invasion of Czechoslovakia on August 21, 1968. The credibility and respect for Russia never recovered. Alexander Dubček (First Secretary of the Czechoslovakia Parliament) and his Action Program for reform were the beginning of the end for communism. Never again would radicals or reformers look to the ruling party to carry out their aspirations or adopt their projects. Communism in Eastern Europe staggered along, sustained by an alliance of foreign loans and Russian bayonets: the rotting carcass was finally carried away in 1989. But the soul of communism died twenty years earlier in Prague, in 1968.

At her time of invasion by fellow Warsaw Pact partners, the Czechs pleaded for help into deaf ears in Washington. The US had a full plate of miseries elsewhere with the expanding war in Vietnam.

For a long time, the increasingly archaic and raggedy Russian bear would continue to face west and occasionally snarl and slash; but it became obvious that the bear was standing on unstable, melting ice. The CIA repeatedly reported that Russia and her satellites were in a steady state of economic decline and moral decay, but no one—either in the West or the East—foresaw that the colossal Russian empire would, like a great iceberg, suddenly and swiftly break up and topple. It would sink into the icy water without a farewell growl while the stubby ghost of First Secretary Nikita Khrushchev watched and choked from his grave over lines from his absurd speech made for the West in 1959 in the Polish Embassy in Moscow, "Whether you like it or not, history is on our side. We will bury you."

Churchill, Roosevelt, and Stalin
Yalta Conference—1945

The Red Army Arrives in Berlin—1945

German Surrender at Stalingrad—1943
Russians—General Rokossovsky; Marshall of Artillery Voronas;
translator, Captain Diatensks—and German Field Marshal von Paulus

CHAPTER 10

POSTWAR WEST GERMANY

Never before had so much been lost—and, yet, never before were there so many new beginnings. Never before had an entire country been rebuilt.
—*Spiegel International*

Back to Normal—1963

When we moved to West Germany to live and work in late 1963, World War II in Europe had been over for eighteen years.

It was sixteen years since the Marshall Plan contributed part of the funding for the remarkable German *"Wirtschaftswunder"* ("economic miracle") making West Germany the center of gravity for European postwar prosperity and currency stability. During the entire mid-1960s the relationship between the value of the Deutschmark and the dollar never varied more than a minor fraction of a percent—four marks to the dollar.

While the US poured Marshall Plan money into Western Europe— especially West Germany—to help with her economic recovery, Russia extracted goods and services of similar value from the countries that she controlled in Eastern Europe. Western European countries soon thrived; Eastern Bloc countries slid into a decades-long depression. The Marshall plan was named for George Marshall, the remarkably talented World War II army chief of staff and postwar secretary of defense and secretary of state.

It was fourteen years since the end of the massive Berlin Airlift. the US flew hundreds of thousands of harrowing flights across one hundred miles of Soviet territory to Berlin's Templehof Airport and two others after Russia cut off ground access to the Western Allies-occupied sectors of Berlin. For eleven months, a "conveyor" of round-the-clock flights—made up largely of four-engine Douglas Skymaster planes—delivered coal, food, medicine, clothing, repair parts, machinery, and military personnel to the beleaguered sectors of the city until Russia was humiliated enough to lift the blockade. When the blockade started, Russia was certain it would cause the Western forces to promptly withdraw from Berlin. Stalin made a major miscalculation of the US's air transportation capabilities—especially in bad winter weather—and her resolve to keep a foothold in Berlin.

I attended engineering college with several older classmates who had flown wartime European bombing missions and the Berlin Airlift flights. They were from a far-off world that was profoundly different from the sophomoric cocoon that most of us lived in. They were serious and mature and seemed to carry dark memories that they did not care to share except with each other. Because of my persistence, they told me a little about the dramatic Berlin Airlift.

It was ten years since the East Germans waged a massive strike and uprising against her Russian occupiers and the failing communist system. After initial confusion, Russia decisively and brutally ended the conflict by sending 20,000 troops, supported with tanks, into Berlin. Beria, the Soviet head of security, advised the troops, "Don't spare the bullets." Russia made it clear that absolute subordination to the wishes and whims of

Moscow were mandatory. The terrified citizens of the sections of Berlin occupied by the Western powers stood by as if they were mice sharing a dance floor with waltzing bears.

It was eight years since Khrushchev allowed the last German POWs—the handful who were still alive—to return home from the brutal Siberian labor camps.

It was two years since West Germany and East Germany officially split into two countries.

And the mortar was barely set-up on the grim, two-year-old Berlin Wall.

In spite of West Germany's rapid economic recovery, all Germans still suffered dreadfully as they went about dealing with the past and finding a new social and physical model for rebuilding their smashed society. And all had to painfully realize that large areas of the eastern sections of prewar Germany were gone forever and the division of the remaining German entity into two separate and very different countries would go on as long as Russia remained the dominant power to the east. Nevertheless, West Germans and most East Germans faithfully held on to the belief that somehow German reunification would eventually come to pass. All thinking West German people also came to realize that West Germany's only hope for viability and security was through an economic and military alliance with the occupying Western forces—especially the US.

Near the end of the war, when defeat by the Allied forces became evident, the throngs of psyched up, cheering German citizens who congregated earlier in gaudily decorated city squares and arenas designed to laud Hitler and the Nazis went silent. The imaginary winged horses drawing gilded chariots with mythical warriors as if they were racing across the domed ceiling of a Vienna opera house vanished as completely as all of the other grand illusions conjured up by the Nazis. In the end, the rousing pageants were replaced with women, children, and wounded ex-soldiers pathetically rooting through the rubble like hungry animals for bits of food to stave off hunger and picking up building material scraps for erecting makeshift shelters.

Egon Bahr, a journalist and politician, foresaw what Germany had in store after the war when he said with gallows humor, "As soldiers we should enjoy the war; the peace will be terrible."

After the war, the country was sundered into a Humpty Dumpty muddle with Russia controlling the East and Great Britain, France, and the US controlling the West. In Berlin, Russia controlled half the city; the rest went to Great Britain, France, and the US. For a long time, as all of the fractious occupying forces deliberated, it seemed the ultimate fate of Germany would be the same as that of Humpty Dumpty:

> All the king's horses and all the king's men
> Couldn't put Humpty back together again.

The problem was aggravated as the "king's horses and men" changed: Roosevelt died from a heart attack and was succeeded by Truman; Churchill was tossed out of office by ungrateful voters and replaced by Attlee; Stalin, replaced by ever-suspicious Khrushchev, sacked Molotov, his minister for foreign affairs, and replaced him with Vishinski. And bewildered France couldn't decide who her horses and men were until she eventually elected imperious, prickly Charles de Gaulle as president in 1959; after that, there was never any ambiguity in anyone's mind about who France's horses and men were.

The confusion, uncertainty, and conflict among the Western Allies over appropriate occupation policies caused grievous suffering in West Germany in the immediate postwar years. Seemingly unanswerable questions often stymied progress: How could Germany feed herself without allowing her industries and trade to resume? Who committed war crimes and what was the appropriate punishment? What were just reparations for countries ravaged by Germany? What did the Germans owe newly formed Israel, the new home for the Jews who survived the Nazi slaughterhouses? Should ex-Nazis be allowed to work in the new government? What should be done about a divided Germany and the loss of large eastern areas to Soviet Bloc countries? What should be the role of the conquerors? What were the military intentions of the powerful and restive Red Army?

Initially the harsh Morgenthau Plan, as envisioned by Henry Morgenthau, Roosevelt's secretary of the treasury, was enforced. The plan called for Germany to become a de-industrialized, pastoral state with people living at the subsistence level. Some dubbed the Morgenthau Plan the "Carthaginian Plan" recalling that ancient Rome leveled the defeated city of Carthage, her archenemy, and allegedly plowed salt into the earth to make it forever barren. Morgenthau wanted to ensure that Germany could never again rearm—likely he was also driven by rage for Hitler's unspeakable torment of the Jews.

In the early 1950s, wiser heads in Washington and London set a new policy that allowed Germany to develop a broad-based economy including the extensive rebuilding of her industries. By then, the US leaders realized that the enemy was no longer Germany; it was Russia and Stalin's aggressive plans for the worldwide expansion of communism. This realization and the brilliantly thought out economic plans of Ludwig Erhard allowed the western part of the divided country to rapidly move forward.

Providing a constant, steadying hand was stalwart Adenauer, who led postwar West Germany for a decade and a half and who never lost faith that most of the German Humpty Dumpty could and would eventually be put back together again. He was a patient man.

For a decade after the war, Austria's fate was similar to that of Germany. Then in 1955 Russian forces withdrew during the "Khrushchev thaw," and after some face-saving horse trading between Russia and the US, Austria again became a free democracy independent from Germany and Russia.

Many Americans thought of themselves as benevolent liberators. This viewpoint was not shared by General Eisenhower, who made it clear that the US military arrived in Germany as a victor, not a liberator. Because of harsh initial occupation policies and individual misbehavior by some US soldiers, Germans clearly understood the US position. They derisively called Americans "*die amis*" (slang for US soldiers).

The chaos and uncertainties after the war and the resettlement of hordes (up to thirteen million) of ethnic Germans pouring into Germany from the East were largely over by the time I arrived. The Nazis, while under the rigid control of Hitler, heavily depended on her talented, well-managed industries. When the war ended and the Nazi political system was destroyed, the intact industrial organizations in West Germany were quickly converted to nonmilitary production with the support of Adenauer's new and enlightened government. In East Germany, the country sunk into the malaise characteristic of the entire communist system of government.

Although the total German workforce—including the millions of refugees from the East—was fully employed, it still was not enough to supply the ravenous manpower needs of the rocketing national economy. The mass importation of foreign *gastarbeiters* (guest workers) to supply additional labor to Germany's humming factories was underway. They came from impoverished Spain, Turkey, Bulgaria, Yugoslavia, Greece, Italy, Poland, the Baltic countries, Romania, Czechoslovakia, Hungary, Morocco, and Tunisia. The Berlin Wall largely stopped the flood of people escaping from tyranny in communist East Germany.

Five hundred Spanish workers lived in barracks and worked in the John Deere Mannheim factory where I worked. Most of them performed nonskilled work such as fork truck driving. More than twenty-five languages were spoken throughout the factory.

When Franz Hamm, a German church leader, observed West Germany's economic miracle, he said, "A ruined, starved, economically depressed and divided Germany, within three years, overcame the economic and social problems posed by millions of people streaming into the country. It was the miracle of the century!"

The economic miracle owed much to the escapees from East Germany. Many were well-educated professionals and skilled farmers fleeing rural collectivism. East Germany suffered severely from the loss of her most valuable human resources.

In 1963 extensive visual evidence of the war still remained throughout West Germany: ruined structures; haphazardly constructed new commercial and residential buildings; abandoned bomb shelters (some stood like ugly, pointy-topped farm silos); choking and blinding pollution (especially where steel mills and coke ovens operated with minimal pollution controls); and substandard housing. In order to get people back on the road as fast as possible, many drove microcars—Isettas with one-cylinder scooter engines and three-wheeled Messerschmitts. A Messerschmitt "lived" at the curb in front of our Handschusheim house. By comparison, our Volkswagen bug looked imposing.

The public would suffer indefinitely from the immediate postwar decisions to speedily rebuild destroyed cities in West Germany. In the haste to rebuild, scant attention was given to planning and reflection. Connections to traditions and history were lost. Architects and builders turned their backs on the soul of older cities with their medieval splendor and charm. Many new concrete building facades looked like gray, monolithic slabs; they were cold and impersonal. Few new postwar structures lifted people's spirits. Frankfurt was one of those cities hastily rebuilt over the ruins of the war. When I went there on business, I was anxious to leave without sightseeing because of its depressing drabness.

In West Germany, factories were running, transportation was operating, communication systems were functioning, the government was stable, and the Deutschmark was the premier European currency. The rapid and effective West German recovery, however, reinforced the worries of many who thought she would soon rearm and again become a menacing military bully. Inimitable Winston Churchill summed up this viewpoint on Germany, "Let her grow fat but stay impotent."

Upon reflection, the victors' worries were unnecessary. After Germany's utter and total defeat, there could be no continuity of the Nazi government after the war. There was no one for her to align with to continue her struggle for territorial expansion. The people were profoundly disoriented and exhausted; survival was their main interest. With Germany's absolute defeat, there was a fundamental break with the past—constitutionally, politically, and psychologically. The Germans called this time in their history *Stunde Null* (zero hour)—the restart time. But there were still those who worried.

Because I was an avid history reader and as a boy closely followed the news media reporting during World War II, I was anxious to add to my knowledge by hearing first-hand accounts from my German colleagues. I soon found this was a naïve expectation. Such discussions were almost always off-limits; the subject was too painful to recall for some; others probably thought I was setting them up for criticism.

However, by listening during my four years in Germany, I heard many people speak—with no prompting from me—of their personal experiences under the Nazi government. I quietly stored their stories away in my memory.

The comradeship among common German soldiers was strong. A colleague spoke of being on the dreaded Eastern Front during the disastrous Battle of Moscow. The one-million-strong German army progressed to the gates of Moscow within binocular sight of the towers of the Kremlin. But when the savage winter arrived like a sledgehammer with its numbing, inescapable arctic wall of ice and snow, the only thought in the minds of the German soldiers was how to survive; it was fifty degrees below zero Fahrenheit. And the soldiers wondered why the army planners did not consider the deadly cold weather that was inevitable in Russian winters. The battle became a meat grinder for the troops of both sides. After Field Marshal Georgy Zhukov (famous for never losing a battle) and his cold-acclimatized troops inflicted a third of a million casualties on the proud Germans, they sullenly retreated. The path of retreat west from Moscow was strewn with snow-covered mounds of frozen soldiers' bodies and the clutter of stalled, non-winterized, tanks, trucks, and weapons. The desolate landscape had earlier been made a wasteland—farms and cities burned, animals slaughtered, crops destroyed, and people exterminated—by the German army when it arrogantly and confidently swept into Russia. The Nazi army's sense of invincibility was now added to the twisted, frozen shambles.

The Russian tolerance for grinding up her troops as well as civilians and captured prisoners was unlimited. General Zhukov used them to shuffle across minefields to explode them and open up safe paths for marching soldiers and tanks. Russian people knew if they retreated, they faced summary death by Red Army bullets. If Russian generals allowed retreat, they were promised a bullet in the head by Stalin.

One of my work colleagues was wounded and fell in the snow in the great battle for Moscow, but his comrades would not leave him to die. They tied him to a sled, wrapped him up, and towed him to safety rather than leave him to his fate on the grim, frozen killing fields outside the Moscow gates.

The strong comradeship among the German soldiers was expressed in a popular and emotional song by Ludwig Uhland:

Once I Had a Comrade

I once had a comrade,
You will find no better.
The drum sounded for battle,
He walked at my side,
In the same pace and step.

A bullet came flying towards us,
Is it meant for me or you?
It tore (swept) him away,
He now lays at my feet,
As if he was a part of me.

His hand reaches out to me,
Meanwhile I am reloading (the rifle).
"I cannot shake your hand (farewell),
You must remain in eternal life (heaven),
My fine (precious) comrade."

When the Red Army went on the offensive against the Germans, it was a time for rage and payback for the earlier inhumane treatment of Russians by the Nazi military. The Russians remembered how the German army encouraged her roops to humiliate and kill people of Slavic heritage because they were *untermenschen* (sub-humans.) The term *untermenschen* was sometimes sarcastically defined by the Nazis as those who were not fortunate enough to have been born into the "master race." It was easier for the soldiers to harm Slavic people if they bought into the harangues of runty (5'-5" tall) Propaganda Minister Göbbels. He said Russians were "like oxen suitable only for providing labor and food.

I heard firsthand stories of the horrible abuse of girls and women by the merciless and vengeful soldiers of the Red Army. A woman acquaintance born in a German community (Sudetenland) of Czechoslovakia, told Rita and me the story of her mother hiding her and her sister in barrels and covering them with potatoes when Russian soldiers were present. Many German women and sometimes entire families committed suicide rather than endure the brutal and often appalling behavior of the Russians.

The soldiers all seemed to know three dreaded words of German: *"frau komm"* (woman, come here) *and "uhri"* (give me your watch). Watch theft by Russian soldiers was a near obsession. A joke made the rounds about a movie news clip in a Hungarian theater showing the famous Yalta Conference with Stalin, Churchill, and Roosevelt. When Roosevelt raised his arm in the film, his wrist watch was visible. A voice in the theater shouted, "Mind the watch!"

A German friend told us that the comportment of American soldiers of occupation—some of whom had experienced poor treatment by the Germans on the battlefields and in captivity—was also not without blemishes. Some GIs indulged in drunkenness, theft, and vandalism.

The behavior of the occupying soldiers shaped the German viewpoint of all of them during the initial postwar years: dread, fear, and hate of the Russians and wariness of the Americans.

Another war memory was recounted by a close German friend who had lived in the US and Australia for ten years after the war. He said that as a boy his father made him accompany him to hear Hitler speak in the Thingstätte Amphitheater, newly built by the Nazis near Heidelberg for use as a place for mass political meetings and glorification of Hitler. As with most boys he did not wish to hear a politician's talk. However, he said, "Hitler mesmerized us. We cheered and jumped about like grasshoppers. We really believed all of the stupid baloney he told us. He was virtually a hypnotist."

When a Deere factory superintendent was asked to make a postwar business trip to France, he bitterly resisted going. He had sour memories of the French for making him perform forced labor on a farm for several years after the war ended. The third time he tried to escape, he succeeded and walked home to Germany. The French and others had the viewpoint that the Germans destroyed much of their country so they should provide the labor to restore it.

A senior John Deere engineering manager did not talk of the war, but his face spoke for him; his cheek and eye were blown away. Hideous war wounds were not uncommon.

I invited a German colleague to accompany me on a visit to a museum for antique cars and farm equipment. He declined because the museum also housed tanks, cannons, and other war machines. The memory of his father's death on the Eastern Front was too vivid and stark to allow him to accompany me to the museum. He quietly waited in the car.

On the other hand, some people wished to talk about their time during the war. A German friend's mother-in-law had married an Austrian who had defected from the Nazis and escaped to the West during the war. He fought in the US Army in Italy. A business trip took us through a Paris suburb where his mother-in-law and her Austrian husband lived. We stopped for a visit and coffee break. He proudly took a tattered and faded picture of himself in a US Army uniform out of his billfold and proudly said, "I fight with Mark Clark's (US military commander in Italy) army." It was more than a quarter of a century since the battles in Italy had ended.

The chief engineer of a Düsseldorf engineering company spoke immaculate British English. He said he learned it in a British prison where he was well treated. The British seemed to quickly downplay the horrors of the war after it ended. Signs beside bombed out ruins in England would typically read, "Destroyed by enemy action on December 10, 1944." The French were less forgiving. On the edge of our company factory in Arc les Gray, France was a sign reading, "On this place, five citizens were executed by the Germans on March 12, 1943."

However, individual British people sometimes showed their continued hatred of the Germans for their destructive wartime bombings and devastation of the country's economy. When I parked my car on a London street, I was vehemently berated by a woman. At first I thought she was deranged, but I understood her actions when she jabbed her umbrella at my car with its German license plate and country identification badge.

Some of the European victors of World War II took manufacturing equipment from Germany back to their countries by the trainload as war reparations—especially the Russians and French. Sometimes they stripped factories of entire production lines down to the concrete floors and carted them away. A Russian official in Berlin ordered, "Take everything out of the eastern section of Berlin; all of it. What you can't take, destroy. Leave nothing; not a single bed, not a chamber pot." A German friend said the managers of his factory anticipated the looting of its heavy metal-forming presses—critical for future operations—so they buried them in the woods and forests for later reclamation.

US industry—not having been destroyed in the war—had no need for German machinery and equipment. They, as well as the Russians and French, took something far more valuable; they took the best German scientists, chemists, biologists, physicists, mathematicians, engineers (especially aeronautics and rocket experts), and strategic technical thinkers to help them with their work on advanced technology.

Werner von Braun, the father of rocketry in Germany, rode his bicycle up to an American army private in Bavaria and surrendered—along with part of his gifted engineering team—in May 1945. He later headed up the spectacular American rocket and space programs. Some berated von Braun for being a Nazi and designing the terrible V-1 and V-2 rockets that indiscriminately destroyed large sections of London and Antwerp. But he had a clear conscience; his passion was only for fundamental space exploration, not war. He worked for the Nazis on military devices as a way to secure funding for engineering and science that could later be transferred to nonmilitary space development.

A German John Deere executive told of his father, Count Schwerin (Ulrich-Wilhelm Graf Schwerin von Schwanenfeld), being brutally killed for participating in the failed plot to assassinate Hitler in July of 1944 and initiate a government coup. The Nazis were less savage to Field Marshall Rommel, a towering war hero implicated in the murder attempt; they let him take poison pills. Schwerin's young sons survived Hitler's vicious, sweeping retribution for the assassination attempt and escaped to a farm in South Africa.

By the mid-1960s, every German must have agonized, in one way or another, over the appalling events of the war and the postwar years. They knew many of them had supported and hailed their *Führer* when he seemed invincible early in the war and even continued after mass bombing, artillery destruction, military failure, and hostile occupation.

But the memories of World War II were starting to fade. The period of postwar chaos was over. It was the first time since before World War I in 1914 that there was peace, prosperity, and stability. It was a time for closure. It was a time to store away the memories and nightmares while awaiting and dreaming of the reunification of all of Germany, but without expectation or hope of ever regaining their prewar eastern provinces: East Prussia, Silesia and most of Pomerania. The foundation for a democratic government was solidly in place but reunification would need to wait for a later generation.

Many people could now move on to more mundane pursuits: fix street potholes, reduce the residential noise levels, set Sunday store opening hours, approve dog leash laws, and improve social services—and worry about the inevitable tax increases needed to pay for their generous social programs.

West German Postwar Minicar

Women Reclaiming Bricks from the Rubble

CHAPTER 11

POSTWAR EAST GERMANY

*It's quite clear—it's got to look democratic,
but we must have everything in our control.*
—Walter Ulbricht, 1945 (leader of communist East Germany)

Kennedy Looking over the Wall to East Berlin—1963

Although East Germany was only several hundred miles from our home in Heidelberg, we saw no reason to go there either for business or personal travel. There was little trade between West Germany and East Germany. Travel to Berlin required the inconvenience of securing a visa and complying with various restrictions. Berlin and the Russian-occupied part of Germany had still not been rebuilt since the war. East Germany was like James Thurber's imaginary childhood attic: a place where mysterious and dangerous things went bump in the night. It was best avoided.

But we could not entirely ignore East Germany. There were too many dangerous threats that could easily escalate into armed conflict. Many feared a minor incident would cause the Western forces to militarily retaliate and precipitate a major clash with Russia and her satellites. The fear never completely subsided.

When East Germany was established in 1949 as a Russian satellite, she called herself the German Democratic Republic (GDR). The term "Democratic" in East Germany meant the ballot offered only one candidate selected by the communist party thereby ensuring he would always win. It was like a horse race with only one horse. Walter Ulbricht, the lowbrow leader of the East German communists, said, "It's got to look democratic, but we must have everything in our control." Beria, head of Russian security, called Ulbricht the "the greatest idiot that ever lived"—but he was the chosen Charlie McCarthy in East Germany with Edgar Bergen pulling the strings and providing the voice from the Kremlin.

Countless East Germans, especially those who were educated and trained, fled to the West before the Berlin Wall was erected. The drain of population was staggering. For the East German government to sustain her sputtering economy, it had to stop the exodus to the West even though it made her look to the rest of the world like she chose to wear a dunce cap and endure ridicule.

East Germany—and her Russian puppeteer—were always front page news and a worrisome concern to West Germany and much of the rest of the world.

Early in World War II, there was a presumption that all of the Western Allies including Russia, were fighting a common battle against Germany with similar postwar goals, including the freedom to choose a form of government and to elect officials of choice. This was true for the US and Britain, but for Russia, the plan was far different. Although the shared objective was to defeat Germany, there was little else in common. Russia only tolerated the Western Allies because they helped her defeat and expel the ravaging German army from her soil.

When the mighty Red Army and the Western forces jubilantly linked up at the end of the war, the victory celebration was fleeting; Stalin issued a strict order to stop all fraternization between the Red Army and "foreigners."

Russia's goal was to establish her totalitarian government system in Germany and the occupied Eastern European countries—later to be known as the Eastern Bloc (Poland, Czechoslovakia, Romania, Austria, the Baltic countries, as much of Germany as possible, Hungary, Bulgaria, Albania, Romania, and Yugoslavia.)

It was not until after the Cold War was in place that the West finally began to understand Russia's totalitarian government system. The stranglehold of Russia was total—much more than even the Nazi government of the Third Reich. All organized activity had to be under the control of the central government—industry, education, religion, political activites, and the media. The communist leaders were suspicious of anything they did not control and dominate.

The Russian totalitarian system also controlled art, poetry, music, dancing, and architecture. It took a lot of twisted thinking to decide the proper communistic version of these subjects. A statue of a robust woman driving a chugging tractor did not lift the spirits of most art enthusiasts.

Being politically neutral in East Germany, Russia, and the Eastern Bloc countries was not acceptable It marked a person as suspicious and subjected him to harassment and often punishment. It was necessary to openly praise communism, rat on nonconformists, attend and cheer at boring speeches, disavow religion, and glorify the working class. To do otherwise was to risk loss of job, denial of medical services, harm to families, and even imprisonment.

The hypocrisy of it all was appalling: constantly tooting horns for the working class, listening to propaganda, sitting through boring nonsensical lectures, bad-mouthing the West, and pretending that living according to the suffocating barebones communistic system and sticking to a disproved economic and political system was paradise. Even rolling of the eyes and frowning during indoctrination sessions was suspect. A sarcastic skeptic said the only means of expressing disapproval of communism was with one's back side because it was concealed by trousers.

The communist authorities in East Germany were plagued by the Voice of America, BBC, and West German radio and television broadcasting. They could not jam it all in their territories. Listeners generally accepted information from these sources as the truth in contrast to the propaganda drummed into them from communist media.

The eyes and ears of the dreaded security forces—the Russian KGB and later the East German Stasi—were everywhere. The "dirt" on every citizen, in minute detail, was retained in voluminous and the threat of persecution was enough to constantly hold people in intense fear of the dreaded knock on the door by the police in the middle of the night. If no negative facts could be revealed, suspicion alone could cause citizens to be branded with the harmful pejorative, "politically unreliable." The communist governments encouraged all citizens to be part of a vast network of stool pigeons and spies.

It was profoundly humiliating and embarrassing for citizens to play this twisted, Orwellian game: control by propaganda, surveillance, misinformation, denial of truth, and manipulation. In this environment, faithful dogs even became suspicious of their masters.

It was necessary for average citizens to feign ignorance and remain silent about the corruption and privileges of party bigwigs who lived in luxurious apartments, owned cars, shopped in stores laden with quality food and merchandise, vacationed in fine resorts, traveled abroad, had access to medical services, and enrolled their children in universities. This hypocrisy was enough to make fellow travelers melt down their hammer and sickle buttons if no one was looking.

It was ironic that in the beginning the people of East Germany had the same work ethic, education, experience, and proven commercial and industrial traditions as those in West Germany. They could have had their own economic miracle had they not been forced to use Russia's fundamentally flawed, tacked-together government policies and crippling communist economic model. The Russian massive occupation forces and meddling Moscow bureaucrats and theoreticians forced the East German people to soil their nests by doing what they knew to be unworkable.

A comparison of East and West Germany overwhelmingly favored the West. The West Germans dug their smashed factories out of the war ruins and quickly set to work making quality products determined by market forces. The same talents in East Germany were compelled to work within the totalitarian communist system and turn out shoddy products with little regard for what the consumer markets desired. It was as if Santa and his elves grew broccoli, mined lumps of coal, and printed books on Marxism in pulp comic book covers for distribution as Christmas presents for the children of the world.

In East Germany, the Russian occupiers left an ugly architectural scene. Entire cities were "scraped" away to make way for large, dull projects. They all looked as if they were designed by the Moscow Department of Public Works with its fondness for hulking, cookie-cutter buildings built around monumental images of communist leaders and stylized factory and farm workers. The large scale of residential and office buildings so dwarfed their surroundings, they were like battleships floating beside rubber duckies in a bath tub. Building quality was poor; walls and roofs leaked; building materials deteriorated; and piping and wiring were an afterthought. Ugly multistory buildings were often built without elevators or adequate kitchens and baths. Heating fuel was polluting, low grade coal. When Germany was reunited, some of the tackier East German buildings were abandoned because of their slipshod nature although they were relatively new.

Never-ending jokes were told about East Germany centered on the smoky, two-cycle engine Trabant car (the "Trabi"): Why do they have heated rear windows? So your hands are warm when you push them. When does a Trabant reach top speed? When it is being towed. And, how do you double the value of a Trabant? Fill up the gas tank. Nevertheless, it took more than ten years of wait time to take delivery of a new Trabant.

One of the worst blunders of the Russian and East German politicians and central planners was to fail to embrace rapidly evolving information technology: silicon chips, computers, software, and hardware. They summarily dismissed it because it would be a challenge to the centralized control of the lives of their people.

Russia designated East Germany to be her principle supplier of high-quality, high-tech equipment to other communist bloc countries. But with Russia's meddling and micromanaging, East Germany failed miserably and fell further behind each year. The freedom, speed, and resourcefulness required in the exploding world of information-related technology baffled the communist *apparatchiks* (bureaucrats.)

I again ran into my previously mentioned eccentric friend at a Heidelberg social gathering. He had recently arrived in Germany from California where he lived in the hippie culture and worked among the information technology geniuses who were starting to call their work community Silicon Valley. His think tank employer paid him to know the status of technology development in the Eastern Bloc countries.

As he sipped his third glass of wine, the muses came to him; he painted an imaginary scene to explain why the Russians could never have a viable information technology industry:

> A couple of dull-witted Russian *apparatchiks* in ill-fitting double-breasted suits work in a Moscow department of advanced technology planning. They hear about the rapidly blooming information technology industry in California that is starting to be called Silicon Valley. They are ordered to invite representatives from California to consult with them on the feasibility of also establishing a modern information technology industry in Russia and her satellites.
>
> For the first meeting, two free-spirited guys from California arrive wearing sandals and kurtas (long-tailed, Indian, shirt-like garments.) They have uncut tangled hair and wispy Ho Chi Minh

beards and are unbathed. They are in an "elevated state of mind" from pot.

They espouse a hippie culture and disdain authority. But they are wickedly smart and fantastically creative. Their Indian guru is sitting cross-legged meditating in their hotel while he waits for the two guys to end the visit.

The California guys explain the status and future of the exploding information technology industry in dizzying technological detail.

They conclude by telling the uncomprehending and dazed *apparatchiks* that for the communists to buy into the California information technology concept, they have to sign on for the "whole deal"—especially the part about total creative freedom to think, work, and live in a free-spirited environment.

As the visitors leave, they hand the bewildered *apparatchiks* a *Whole Earth Catalogue* with its counterculture theme and disturbing ideas for radically transforming the world.

The free-wheeling, fantastically creative, "chip-head guys" from California have the same chance to receive an invitation for a return visit as a wolf would have for a lunch invitation from Little Red Riding Hood and her grandmother.

Although we enjoyed my friend's story that stretched poetic license to the limit, most of us had little more understanding of the coming information technology revolution than the Russian *apparatchiks*.

Most of the clueless, geriatric Russian politburo members rigidly called the shots from the isolation of the Kremlin and their posh country dachas. Rigid, unimaginative adherence to the party line was a prerequisite for political career advancement and it always trumped imaginative thinking. The words from a John Dryden satirical poem about a newborn child suggest a reason why the dullards in the Russian government could not understand and accept the fast-moving advancements underway in the West:

> The Midwife laid her hand on his thick skull
> With this prophetic blessing, 'Be Thou Dull.'

Although Berlin, surrounded by communism, was the East German capital, it remained, in the imagination and dreams of all Germans, a mystical and colorful epicenter for spirited culture, avant-garde art, flourishing intellectual happenings, advanced thinking, progressive music, lively entertainment, creative writing, publishing, political stirring, and dynamic discourse. It was a kind of an informal clearing house between the East and the West. It was like a water lily still able to bloom even in the fetid pond of stifling communism. Anneliese Bödecker, a Berlin social worker said, "Berlin is repulsive, loud, dirty, and grey. Construction work and blocked streets are everywhere. But I feel sorry for those people who cannot live here!"

The Germans bided their time waiting for the day of reunification and the rebirth of a throbbing, vibrant Berlin.

The separate establishment of diametrically opposed governing systems in West and East Germany was like a giant laboratory for giving the world a chance to test and examine the two systems in the full light of day—freedom and democracy versus totalitarianism and extreme socialism. And to compare the abundance of high-quality food and products versus limited availability of palatable food and drab merchandise. The test would be long and convoluted. The Russians would welcome the test in the same way that creatures under rocks accept sunlight. They would not fare well with the test; communism would utterly fail. The end result, although long in coming, would be as final and unambiguous as the dropping of the trap door on a hangman's scaffold.

Berlin Airlift—1948

Removing Body of Defecting East German
from Barbed Wire Fence in Berlin

CHAPTER 12

POSTWAR NIGHTMARES

*A thousand years will pass and
the guilt of Germany will not be erased.*
—Hans Frank (hung for war crimes)

*We had gambled, all of us, and lost: lost Germany, our country's
good repute and a considerable measure of our personal integrity.*
—Albert Speer (from his prison diary)

*The memory of the war and the genocide are part of our life. Nothing
will change that: these memories are part of our national identity.*
—Chancellor Gerhard Schröder, 2005

*Events will take their course, it is no good being angry at them;
he is happiest who wisely turns them to the best account.*
—Euripides, 450 BC

Buchenwald Concentration Camp—1944
Liberation Day

Although the postwar rebuilding of the West German government and economy was contentious and difficult, it was far easier than dealing with the psychological monster that lived just under the skin of most German people. The monster was the inexplicable nature of their behavior as a people and as individuals before and during World War II.

A moral German intellectual reflected on his country's conduct during the Nazi era with these words:

> We were a proud people where beacons from around the world shone on our traditions of culture, learning, and achievement. And yet we fell—while we were in complete control of our destiny—into a black hole of shame.

Martin Niemöller, a prominent Lutheran pastor, who spent five years in Nazi concentration camps, wrote:

First they came for the Communists, and I did not speak out
because I was not a Communist.
Then they came for the Trade Unionists, and I did not speak out
because I was not a Trade Unionist.
Then they came for the Jews, and I did not speak out
because I was not a Jew.
Then they came for me, and there was no one left to speak for me.

There were many others—including officials at the highest levels in the German government and military—who denied any personal responsibility for Germany's disgraceful mass genocide of various categories of people with the smug explanation, "I just followed orders." In the late 1940s, at the highly publicized Nuremberg War Criminal Trials of high-ranking Nazis, their frequent defense plea was *Befehl ist Befehl* (an order is an order.) This gave rise to the term "Nuremberg Defense."

None of Nazi officials on trial remembered or accepted the lessons of their university philosophy professors who lectured on the writings of the ancient scholars and their belief that there is a fundamental moral code that cannot be trumped by the orders of man.

On the other end of the spectrum from the generals, admirals, titans of industry, and government ministers were the everyday military combatants, who usually viewed themselves as powerless when they were forced to fight under unimaginable conditions and compelled to commit cold-blooded atrocities. They wondered why they should carry any guilt at all for the terrible deeds of the Nazis and others. Having suffered physically and mentally themselves, they carried a strong sense of victimhood and rested easily with the knowledge that they had honorably done their duty when called upon to serve their country. Most of them also did not consider respecting the higher moral code.

Hitler and the Nazis held their highest scorn and contempt for the Jews, Gypsies, Jehovah Witnesses, homosexuals, and handicapped. Then came the conquered Slavic people to the east. They dished out their worst abuse, however, to the Jewish population.

The Nazis set up most of their concentration camps in the East to be "utilized" for the native populations as well as for those "drafted" from the West. They transported victims to the camps in railroad cars as if they were rubbish being hauled to a dump. The deaths in the railroad cars from crowding and cold recalled the incident at the Black Hole of Calcutta two centuries earlier where many British soldiers perished from being jammed into a tiny, black jail room. Those who arrived "safely" (alive) at the concentration camps perished in gas chambers or were worked to death and disposed of in crematoriums and mass graves. By placing most of the killing camps in the East, it was not necessary to "sully German soil."

The profound irony of Hitler's twisted view of the Jewish peoples is this: The Jews were the very people who might have allowed him to prevail with his plans for dominating all of Europe. They were the heavyweights in developing the scientific theories that became the basis for nuclear weapons: Albert Einstein, Robert Oppenheimer, Niels Bohr, Edward Teller, and John von Neumann. Most of them came to the US from Europe to dodge the gas chambers and bullets of the Nazis. Their towering and imaginative intellects, along with the involvement of many other scientists, shook the world of science and raised the threat of the biblical Armageddon. If the Nazis had developed nuclear weapons, they likely would have succeeded with their plans for domination of Europe. Hitler derisively referred to nuclear research and development as "Jewish Physics."

A friend, who lived as a boy throughout the war in Mannheim, told me, "We knew the Jews were having a difficult time, but we did not know of their mass extermination."

Some people wondered if many Germans "conveniently" remained ignorant of the terrible truth about the disappearance and fate of Jews and other "undesirables." The consequence of them knowing that the Nazis behaved so badly toward "undesirable" fellow citizens could have profoundly shattered their elevated images of German cultural, social, intellectual, and moral standards and made their continued support of the Nazi government and the war difficult or impossible. Some claimed the

German people indulged in a self-induced epidemic of collective amnesia about the dark times of the war.

Many Nazis thought that when they killed the Jews en masse, they had "cleared the ground" and forever expunged all vestiges of their presence on earth. Little did they know that the surviving Jews throughout the world would relentlessly immortalize Nazi abuses by endlessly writing and speaking of the Holocaust; it would become an entire industry. George Bailey, a historian, writes that the Holocaust makes Jews "the elite of sufferers."

I observed that the German people were more inclined to speak of their own suffering during and after the war than of the brutal suffering the Nazis had caused others. The memories of wartime deeds were likely so wicked for some, the atrocities were best "mis-remembered."

After the war, most German citizens did not accept universal condemnation by the conquering Allies. The following comments characterize the variety of opinions held by many Germans:

> We are the real victims of the war under the heel of the Nazis. We are now being judged retroactively by the laws of occupying countries and nebulous international laws. Germany should rebuild her military strength to help face the mounting Russian threat. Why should we constantly relive the Nazi horrors? Let's forget it and enjoy the prosperity from the improving economy. We have already atoned enough by enduring the vengeful allied bombings of our cities—especially Dresden—that had no military sifnificance. Why deny jobs to the talented professional and administrative people—even if they are ex-Nazis—whom we need to rebuild our country's infrastructure and manage our government?
>
> It is sanctimonious for Americans to so harshly criticize Germans considering her history of abuse to Native Americans and African Americans. And Great Britain should remember her oppression of the citizens of her colonies. And citizens of German-occupied territories—France, Holland, Norway, Belgium, Russia, and other countries—should recall their collaboration with the Nazis in rounding up their Jewish citizens for extermination.
>
> The atrocities committed by the Nazis were not the doing of the German public at large. Prolonging the denazification process and denying amnesty to tens of thousands of able and talented people is a crippling distraction from the burden of building a new democratic government as it faces the opportunities and perils of the future. Germany must rebuild her security forces

(military), but this cannot happen until prosecutions end and honor and respect are restored to the common soldiers and officers from the wartime years.

Many people outside Germany—and some Germans—believed the Nuremberg trials were a fitting requiem for strutting Nazi leaders who proclaimed that the Third Reich would last a thousand years. (It lasted twelve.) Eleven high-level Nazi officials who were tried for war crimes at Nuremberg received death sentences; several bit into cyanide pills before they could be hanged.

Many influential politicians and legal scholars believed the decisions of the Nuremberg tribunals would not hold up well in the light of history. They said the trials were an attempt to establish a new world order based on responsibility to international law—whatever the trial judges and lawyers believed international law was.

A Nuremberg trial observer who knew the early history of "justice" in Ireland from British courts—with their foreign language and laws—recalled a line spoken by an Irishman in the dock (on trial), "I feel like an insect in a court of birds."

Some Germans—including future West German chancellors Adenauer and Erhard—had no involvement with the Nazis; they felt they carried no responsibility or collective guilt whatsoever related to the horrors of the Nazi regime. They devoted all of their resources to cleaning up the postwar mess in Germany, restoring national pride, trying to reunite West and East Germany, quietly providing economic aid to fledgling Israel, and setting a democratic course for the structure and politics of the country that would squelch any more beer hall hallucinations about the Germans being an Aryan master race ordained by the gods to rule the world.

Other German people assumed the traditional attitude of defense lawyers by denying everything that was unfavorable to their case. The US Department of War created an education movie, *Die Todesmühlen* (The Death Mills) to educate the German public on some of the twisted criminal behavior of the Nazis. It focused on concentration camp scenes with the intent of shocking the viewers. The comments of two men as they departed a movie theater were recorded. One said, "Do you think it will snow tonight"? The other said, "It's all American (*Ami*) propaganda" as if he had just viewed a Hollywood soap opera.

A few haughty and unrepentant Nazis still believed if they had not been betrayed by Hitler and his incompetent henchmen, they would have prevailed with their plans for dominating all of Europe. They continued to trust in the wisdom of Hitler's policy for "culling out" the Jews and other "undesirables" and leaving a "purified Aryan race" of inherently superior people. They futilely bided their time until they could rise again.

Occasionally the guilt nightmares from the war passed on to later generations. In the 1980s, I talked to a young barmaid in my Heidelberg hotel who was the granddaughter of a German war veteran. She said, "Why, when I was not born during the time of the Nazis and the war, must I be tormented with these never-ending feelings of guilt?" She became so distressed and agitated about the issue of war guilt that we left the bar rather than watch her anguish.

The most prevalent viewpoint that slowly evolved on sharing the guilt for inhuman Nazi behavior was simply this: Ordinary citizens, soldiers, officers, and state officials who did not directly participate in criminal acts should not be expected to bear a guilt load. The heavy load should be carried by the Nazis in top leadership roles and those in lesser positions if they committed flagrant crimes.

For younger people, the period just after the war was a profoundly wrenching time. The preposterous Nazi propaganda had been hammered into them since childhood. Now they learned it was false and in many instances evil. In the postwar chaos, they felt like they were in swirling flood waters while desperately trying to find something to hang onto.

Some embraced the teachings of Marx and Lenin with their rosy promises of order, equity, and happiness. Communism as a form of government would remain credibile in many western countries for many decades before its nonviability and corruption would be revealed.

Judging the degree of guilt for each individual who lived and participated in the German wartime era would have stumped the Wisdom of Solomon. Lenient amnesties were finally granted to thousands of Germans with the implication that—when uncertainty existed—final judgments would be made and appropriate punishment meted out in the next world. An historian recalled a line from Abraham Lincoln's second inaugural address where he tried to set the tone for healing after the carnage of the American Civil War, "Only the judgments of the Lord are true and righteous."

Each German citizen personally dealt with the nightmarish memories of the Third Reich's criminal behavior in his own way. Some accepted personal responsibility; some blamed it all on others; and some denied that atrocities—such as the Holocaust—ever happened. The Germans were not unique with their denials. the Turks still deny they massacred over a million Armenians in World War I, and the Japanese often ignore and deny their atrocities in World War II.

Some thought they owed gratitude to the Third Reich for the "benefits" to them by its ethnic cleansing policies. They said they were betrayed by their politicians, and that they were really the aggrieved ones. In order to sleep at night, a few were able to sweep it all into the "dead compartments" of their minds. Many said, although they were ashamed of the behavior of the German people, they felt no personal guilt for actions with which they had no control or involvement.

The Germans were not alone with their record of atrocities to the Jews and others. The citizens of many occupied territories were complicit in helping identify and capture victims for extermination.

In Vichy France (the half of the country controlled by the local French government that was a puppet for the Nazis), the authorities willingly did all of the Germans' governing and dirty work for them thereby freeing up thousands of German administrators and security forces to do their nasty work elsewhere. Only occupied Denmark did not cooperate in rounding up "undesirables;" most of her Jewish population survived.

When Germans read this book, some will probably recall how much they also suffered from the relentless Allied bombing of their nonmilitarized cities and civilians as if they were cereal grain being ground under a millstone. They will likely say the bombings were immoral, indiscriminate, and totally disproportionate to the earlier German raids on Allied cities. They will explain that mostly harmless women, children, and elderly people perished and that the priceless artwork and ancient architectural monuments destroyed were treasures for the entire world. They will possibly also recall that when Hitler ordered the burning of beautiful and historic Paris near the end of the war, his retreating commanders refused because they did not want to be remembered for destroying a world treasure.

But no matter how people slice up blame for the reeking, dead carcass of the Third Reich, the time that it existed probably will go down in history as the low point for humans' presence on earth.

History is not mute; what happened will not change and it will never go away no matter how much it is shrouded, explained, rationalized, and denied. The long, dark shadow of World War II will lay over Germany and Europe indefinitely.

After the war ended Hannah Arendt, a writer, coined the phrase, "the banality of evil" to describe and explain the behavior of some of the worst Nazis actions. In 1963, she concluded her book about the trial of Adolph Eichmann, a major organizer of the Holocaust, by writing, "He carried out a policy for not sharing the earth with Jewish people and the people of a number of other nations—as though it was his and his superior's right to determine who should and who should not inhabit the earth. We find no one, that is no member the of human race, can be expected to want to share the earth with Eichmann."

It is nearly impossible to find a suitable explanation for the evil behavior of Hitler and the Nazis. The classical Greeks devised stories to explain the unexplainable. The ancient myth of Pandora's box may be compelling enough to explain Hitler and the Nazis. Pandora, a woman of sheer guile and ethereal beauty, was entrusted by the god, Zeus, to be the keeper of a container that held all of the evils of mankind. Overcome by her curiosity, Pandora opened the box and released its evils into the world. Hitler could be imagined to be the personification of the evil in Pandora's box and his spirit could be envisioned to be eternally doomed to travel up and down the face of the earth while people point to him with the finger of scorn.

But also—according to the Greek myth—hidden under the lid of Pandora's box was hope. And hope was the foundation upon which enlightened postwar Germans were rebuilding their dreams for the future of their country.

By the late 1960s, many thought it was time to move forward and heed Jane Austen's optimistic words from her novel of a century earlier, "Let other pens dwell on guilt and misery."

More than six decades later after research and reflection, much of Europe has finally accepted and memorialized the agonizing memories of the wicked events of the Nazi era. Museums and monuments have been erected throughout Europe.

In Berlin, adjacent to the Brandenburg Gate, stands an imposing memorial unambiguously named, "Memorial to the Murdered Jews of Europe." In Paris "The Deportation Memorial" states, "Dedicated to the living memory of the 200,000 French deportees sleeping in the night and fog, exterminated in the Nazi concentration camps." At the memorial exit is written, "Forgive but never forget." In Budapest a Holocaust museum is named *TerrorHaza* (House of Terror.)

Other old and new memorials to the horrors and terrorism of World War II also exist throughout Europe. Some have recently been revised to remove the earlier twisting of facts on the memorial placards. Poland was treated especially badly by the Nazis and the Russians during the war, but she also has a dark record of her own. Controversial World War II memorials in Poland are still being sorted out.

But memorials and words on museum placards can never adequately cleanse haunting memories from human souls any more than tombstones and commemorative endowments can ease the tormenting pain of parents of innocent children taken by depraved killers.

Nuremberg Nazi War Criminal Trial
Hermann Göring, Rudolph Hess, Joachim VonRibbentop,
and Wilhelm Keitel

Memorial to the Murdered Jews of Europe
Near Brandenburg Gate in Berlin

CHAPTER 13

TRAVELING IN EUROPE

I think that travel comes from some deep urge to see the world, like the urge that brings up a worm in an Irish bog to see the moon when it's full.
—Lord Dunsany

Dubrovnik, Yugoslavia
Adriatic Sea Coast

As soon as the German people again stabilized their lives after the war, they were able to indulge their passion for travel and sightseeing. Even with lean postwar budgets, they soon found a way to vacation by camping and carrying their own food and drinks. A technician who worked in our Mannheim foundry office acquired a small car that he and his family used for their first vacation. They went to the lakes of northern Italy. They were as happy as children with their first bicycles.

147

Rita and I had a similar passion for travel and sightseeing; we toured Western Europe as much as possible during our three-week annual vacations and on long weekends and holidays. With the strong dollar, our fuel-efficient Volkswagen, and our reliance on a popular travel book, *Europe on Five Dollars a Day*, we could poke through a lot of territory on a limited budget. The sights were no less beautiful even when our budget was tight.

Although our Volkswagen was small, so were our children; John could stretch out and sleep in the space between the back seat and the rear window; it was his Pullman berth. Kathy could stretch out on the back seat.

Sometimes our children went with us and sometimes they stayed at home in Heidelberg. At times, Frau Wörle, our faithful housekeeper, cared for them. When she did, Kathy insisted that we instruct her not to cook a dish she made with a type of sausage that she disliked. At other times they stayed in the homes of Rita's many friends—often with a reciprocal agreement to care for their children or let their guests live in our unused, third-floor rooms.

The children's favorite place to stay while we were on vacations without them was the home of American friends with four rambunctious teenagers whom we paid for their "baby-sitting" services. The boys threw the children in the air and taught them the latest trendy teenage ditties and goofy jokes. For weeks after our return we heard, "Hit ya motha with ya brotha! Ooh! Ahh!"

Although our children often traveled with us in an agreeable manner, there were times when we recalled the observation of Robert Benchley when he wrote, "Taking a trip with children is roughly like travelling third class on a Bulgarian railroad."

Switzerland—only several hours away—was often our destination for vacations or holiday weekends. It escaped the damage and chaos of World War II. It has some of the most spectacular terrain in the world. The quaint villages and "too-perfect" mountain sides are sites for chalets suitable for the homes of Heidi and Peter. Some of the mountain crags house monasteries with monks who look like they are reincarnations of Old Testament Biblical Prophets.

Selecting which of four official languages to speak in Switzerland was a challenge. German is common in the north. It is written in standard High German but is commonly spoken in a dialect that I could never understand. French and Italian are spoken in areas adjacent to France and Italy. A handful of people speak Romansh, an ancient Latin-based language. In exquisitely beautiful Lucerne, shopkeepers do not want to linguistically offend either their French- or German-speaking clients; they wish them off after a purchase with a cheerful *Merci vielmals* (thank you in French and very much in German).

Rita's high school mate who had been a wartime refugee in the US moved back to her family's home and business in Bruges, Belgium after the war. She and her large family (six children) owned a weekend house—the Flemish Bonnet—a few miles away from Bruges on the wide, spotless North Sea beach in Zeebrugge. For our first visit to Zeebrugge, we traveled on the Trans-Europe Express train, a four-hour ride from Heidelberg. Six-year-old Kathy was impatient on the trip so we let her run in the train aisle. When she looked out the window, she saw a herd of cows and exclaimed, "*Ach du lieber heiliger Strohsack*"—a nonsense expression of surprise literally meaning, "Oh, dear, holy straw mattress!" Her fractured German amused the passengers and astonished us because Kathy was not enthusiastic about her German classes.

Our frequent visits to Zeebrugge were great fun for our children. The white, packed-sand beaches were a fine racetrack for them on self-propelled go-carts.

It was a surprise to find resort beach living and seaside recreation within sight of the great cargo ship and ferry terminal in the Port of Zeebrugge. The traffic was largely to and from Great Britain—a several hour trip. A few years after our last visit, a car and passenger ferry set out from Zeebrugge to England with its car ramp inexplicably left open. One kilometer from shore it sank in icy water. Half of its four hundred passengers drowned or died of hypothermia.

At our host's dinner table, there were always three languages underway simultaneously: Flemish (similar to Dutch), English, and French. The visits were fun-filled and a good way to sample the rich Belgian culture.

Our host liked to poke fun at the Belgian reputation for never opening purses to daylight. He told the story of two frugal Belgians who invented electric wire when they both simultaneously picked up a copper coin from the street. After their tug-of-war to determine ownership of the coin, they had stretched it into fine copper wire suitable for conducting electric current.

When we visited nearby Netherlands, one of the engineers who worked in our foundry group was in The Hague, his hometown, for a weekend. He invited us to his parents' house beside a canal for tea.

The horrors the family endured from hunger and the atrocities of the Nazi occupiers were still fresh in their minds. All food was embargoed and thousands starved during the last winter of the war. The Nazis set up the embargo in retaliation for Dutch sympathy toward the approaching, liberating Western Allied Forces. They called it the *Hongerwinter* (hunger winter.)

Our hosts also told us of an old deaf man peddling his bicycle on the street in front of their house during the war. A German soldier told him to stop so he could confiscate his bicycle. Because of deafness, the old man did not stop; the soldier shot him in the back. In spite of the Nazi atrocities, the Dutch showed their wry humor after the war by hanging out banners asking, "When will we get our bicycles back?" They also greeted German vacationers with a sign, "Welcome to the Netherlands. But this time go back home in two weeks."

The wife of our host had an equally bad story to tell of her six-year childhood internment along with her parents in a Japanese prison camp in Indonesia. Her father died of malnutrition during the detention.

Northern Italy was always a great place for vacations—especially watery Venice with her extravagant Byzantine and Arab-influenced architecture, bridges, palaces, canals, gondolas, churches, and art glass.

We bought an ornate secretary (desk) from a Venetian street vendor. Without a common language, we negotiated and made shipping arrangements with exaggerated gesticulations and wild hand-waving signals. The shipping mode to our house in Heidelberg was difficult to establish until Rita rushed around pumping her arms up and down while making "choo-choo" and "huff-puff" sounds. We naively paid for the secretary based on trust that it would be delivered. And it was!

The Venetians are experts at body language and hand gesture communications. From a distance, we watched a group of gondola builders "talking" Venetian style. Until we came closer, we thought they were deaf people signing among themselves.

A day of walking along the canals; resting in a pew in exotic, mosaic-tiled St. Mark's Basilica and perhaps lighting a votive candle for a departed loved one; looking in shops with their extravagant glassware; paddling on the canals in gondolas; crossing lagoons in vaporetti (steam boats); touring the Palace of the Doge; and taking late afternoon refreshments in an elegant arcade restaurant while listening to orchestral music gave us the feeling that we were participants in an elaborate Italian opera. Even the "imagineering" teams of Walt Disney would not have had the imagination to invent Venice.

We traveled several times to Rome. My most memorable and moving moment was walking on the finely preserved, 2,300-year-old Appian Way near Rome. The superbly built, two-carriage-wide road was built for the fast deployment of the Roman legions. It was also the place where six thousand slaves revolted and were crucified and hung at the curbs like hideous rows of scarecrows.

I felt like I was time-machined back and surrounded by history as I stood in the sunshine and read on a stone marker, *Appia tentur regina longarum viarum* (the Apian Way is the queen of long roads). The Roman road engineers would have been proud if they could have looked ahead two millennia and seen the continent-spanning US Interstate Highway System that was partly inspired by the Appian Way.

Bavaria with her pastoral countryside, onion-domed churches, quaint villages, and alpine settings was one of our frequent travel destinations. Every ten years, in Oberammergau, the Passion Play is dramatically re-enacted to recall a desperate promise made centuries earlier to honor Christ if the town was spared the bubonic plague epidemic that killed half of the European population; the plague by-passed Oberammergau. The pageant draws tens of thousands of visitors from around the world.

Many house and building exteriors in Oberammergau are painted with frescoes showing religious scenes from the Passion Play; fairy tales, especially the story of Little Red Riding Hood; and traditional nature scenes—deer, cows, pine trees, birds, and mountains.

The hallmark of Bavaria is the unfinished fantasy castle of King Ludwig; it attracts millions of visitors annually. Castle tours are usually supplemented with stories about the weirdness of Ludwig and his life as he lived it in his fairyland imagination. His unconventional lifestyle, extravagant castles, reclusiveness, agony in dealing with his sexual orientation, and mysterious death all could have been scenes from his friend Richard Wagner's complex and dramatic operas.

On a visit to Bavaria, Rita and I made a side visit to a place that Dante could not have imagined for the worst ring of hell in his epic work *The Inferno*. We visited the Dachau concentration camp museum with its famous cynical sign over the entry gate, *Arbeit macht frei* ("Work makes you free"). For its prisoners who labored in the camp and starved to death, it really meant, "Work makes you dead." Several crematorium ovens remained as they were first discovered by the incredulous troops of the liberating US Seventh Army.

The camp was the first of its kind and a prototype for many others. During its ten-year existence, 200,000 people died of overwork, exposure, starvation, hideous medical experiments, death marches, shooting, and gassing. The people who died—those on the Nazi list of "undesirables"—were as varied as the method for killing. We drove home in stunned silence and could think of little else for days.

In contrast, a visit to the beautiful parts of Bavaria—and also nearby Austria—was an experience to be repeated whenever possible; it was a treat to the mind, the ears, the eyes, and the taste buds. It was an opportunity for renewing the spirits.

Also a "visit again" place for us was the Cotswold area of England with her quaint village names: Bourton-on-the-Water; Chipping Norton; Stow-on-the-Wold; Burford, Horsley; Upper Slaughter, Lower Slaughter, and Cirencester. The communities were built in medieval times with wealth from the wool trade.

Our favorite place to stay in the ancient Cotswold Hills was in The Shaven Crown Inn in the tiny village of Shipton-Under-Wychwood. Originally it was a Benedictine monastery and later a hunting lodge for Queen Elizabeth I.

Our waiter in the old inn restaurant had worked there since boyhood. His signature remark to every guest at every contact was a curt "cue." Sixty years earlier the word started out as "thank you." Ten minutes before closing time, he made it clear it was time for the guests to depart the dining room when he snapped on his bicycle-riding pant clips.

Street lighting was sparse in the small Cotswold villages; night darkness was total. Apparently it always was a problem. A public notice—written long ago with remarkable clarity—reported that an unfortunate man, William, endured a fatal concussion of the brain when he fell off his horse while riding home after nightfall from a day at the ancient Malmesbury Fair. The notice suggest two possible reasons for the fall: the horse may have stumbled in the dark or William's brain might have been dulled by drink. The notice ends by informing the reader, "William enjoyed the Malmesbury Fair but it was the last one he would ever attend."

In the Cotswolds, it was hard to define where nature ended and man-made structures began. The cottages were built of rustic local limestone and roofed with native split-slate or stone shingles or sometimes with honey-colored thatch.

Every path, field, village, cottage, church, bridge, stream, stone fence, and sheep paddock was a treat for the eye. A frequent visitor said, "When I hike through the Cotswolds, I feel like a one-eyed dog in a meat market."

Although our daughter, Kathy, was a child when she vacationed with us in the Cotswolds, she never forgot the beauty of the area. More than a decade later, when she selected a place to practice teach for her university education degree, she chose Cirencester in the Cotswolds. The food in the community sounded quaint to American ears; Kathy's landlady, Mrs. Robinson, often served her "bubble and squeak" (leftovers) for Sunday supper.

Most of our trips to Great Britain included a few days in London. We loved to walk the streets of the city, especially Threadneedle Street, the financial center of the British Empire, past the Bank of England (the Old Lady of Threadneedle Street). The district was defined by the uniform attire of the bankers and financial institution employees: mutton chop whiskers, black derby hats, and camel hair overcoats. They showed as much individuality as a rookery of penguins.

I would betray my Irish heritage if I did not write of our many visits to Ireland. Ireland and Germany have a long history of connection. After invading Vandal tribes sacked Rome and ravaged her civilization in the fifth century, continental Europe huddled in intellectual darkness for centuries while Ireland simultaneously had her golden age. Four centuries later pious and scholarly Irish monks brought back learning, art, mathematics, classical languages, philosophy, and Christianity to the continent. A ninth century European observer wrote, "Almost all of Ireland is migrating to our shores with a herd of philosophers." Occasionally the monks' enlightened teachings did not go down well; an Irish philosophy teacher was stabbed to death by his students' pens when he mocked their belief in superstition and magic.

During World War II, the tacit attitude in neutral Ireland toward Germany was ambivalence; anyone who opposed the British was not entirely without virtue.

When we traveled in Ireland in the 1960s, it was only a few years since she had separated from Great Britain, and a degree of rebuilding was starting after centuries of subjugation and neglect. Although there was still ample evidence of physical deprivation, there was no deficiency of spirit and humor.

We walked on O'Connell Street in Dublin in 1966 on the day after an IRA (Irish Republican Army) group blew to smithereens the statue and tall, supporting pillar of legendary British naval hero and notorious adulterer, Admiral Horatio Nelson, who never met an opposing navy that he did not sink. He cast his left eye and pointed this left index finger (he lost his right eye and right arm in naval battles) over the broad boulevard from atop his pillar for more than a century and a half and provided a safe perch for generations of pigeons. Apparently the IRA group did not think Nelson's legendary naval exploits and advice to his sailors—"England expects that every man will do his duty"—had relevancy in Ireland. The demolition of Nelson's dominating statue was the Irish way to commemorate the fiftieth anniversary of the 1916 Irish uprising against eight centuries of British occupation and oppression.

Rita, with her puckish humor, turned to a young Irish policeman standing near the shattered heap of Nelson's remaining body parts, the pillar, and shower of accumulated pigeon droppings and asked, "Officer, now would blowing up Lord Nelson's statue last night be regarded as an illegal act"?

He immediately picked up on the drift of her question when he replied, "That, Madam, could be one viewpoint."

A few weeks later, a song sung to the tune of "The Battle Hymn of the Republic," became the hit song of Ireland:

Up Went Nelson

One early mornin' in the year of '66
A band of Irish laddies were knockin' up some tricks
They thought Horatio Nelson had overstayed a mite
So they helped him on his way with some sticks of gelignite.

Up went Nelson in old Dublin
Up went Nelson in old Dublin
All along O'Connell Street the stones and rubble flew
As up went Nelson and the pillar too.

The hurried departure of Nelson from his pillar provoked Eamon De Valera to suggest a headline for the Irish Press, "Lord Nelson left Ireland airborne last night." It was the only recorded instance of humor from the stern Irish revolutionary and political leader.

The remains of Nelson's pillar soon became known as "The Stump." Nelson's statue was eventually succeeded by a tall, steel object, officially called "The Spire of Dublin." It looks like the world's biggest toothpick.

Rather than "foreign" military figures, Ireland preferred to honor her great poets, writers, orators, politicians, and singers: Yeats, Joyce, Swift, Shaw, Burke, Wilde, McCormack, Heaney, Parnell, and Synge. To visit the Dublin Writer's Museum often required standing in line.

After we spent an evening in the sanctuary of a nearby pub for a few draughts of Guinness and wee drops of Jameson, we were surrounded by the imaginary presence of our forebears: Donohoe, Lyons (Lehan), Beecher, Dwyer, Peters, Burns, Coughlin, Donlan, Crossgrove, Finley, Whelan, Maloney, O'Connor, and Kinney. As the evening lengthened and the swirling vapors of the night thickened, our forebears even seemed to talk, recite, and sing to us.

After the Republic of Ireland regained her sovereignty, the predominately Catholic citizens—in baffling contradiction—no longer gave a fig about the nationality, religion, or affiliation of any of her citizens. Robert Briscoe, a Jew, became the Lord Mayor of Dublin and two Protestants, Douglas Hyde and Erskine Childers, became presidents of Ireland.

We visited an ancient Protestant church with old and beautiful stained glass windows. I talked to the church sexton and inquired about the need for security against possible vandalism of the windows. He said, "Now, Saar (Sir), why in the world would anyone want to bring harm to windows as foin (fine) as these?"

The six counties of Northern Ireland, with their majority Protestant population, remained part of Great Britain after the twenty- six counties of the Republic of Ireland to the south became independent. For decades "The Troubles" (conflict between the two Irelands) flamed high in the north with ever-accelerating terror tactics, fighting, bombing, and assassinations.

Firebrand Reverend Ian Paisley fired up his pack of braying rabble rousers when he called the Pope "The whore of Babylon" and said the Irish Catholics were "Rabbits that breed like vermin." The Protestant citizens egged on ill-feelings by annually marching and singing through Catholic neighborhoods to celebrate their victory in the Battle of the Boyne in 1690. Catholics, who were fewer in number in Northern Ireland, taunted and provoked the Protestants and British peace-keeping soldiers at every opportunity. And none was shy about shooting and bombing those on the other side.

The quest to recombine all of Ireland into a single sovereign republic would continue to be a cause for violence and bloodshed for many more decades.

Old grievances were long remembered and often settled with grim retribution. W. B. Yeats, the poet voice of Ireland, expressed the sentiments of many Irish people on the need for violent intervention to expel the British from Ireland in his poem:

The Rose Tree
(Symbol for Ireland)

When all the wells are parched away
O plain as plain can be
There's nothing but our own blood
Can make a right Rose Tree.

The physical beauty of Ireland is varied, lush, and awesome, but it is secondary to the stirring beauty of spoken words, songs, conversations, poetry, and writing.

I never visited Ireland that I did not also recall it was a "terrible beauty" to again use the disturbing words of Yeats. It was as if lovely words and songs would hide and heal the aching wounds and brooding memories of the past: bogus imprisonment, forced emigration, famine, injustice, violence, oppression, and sorrow. It also occurred to me that if the names and dates were changed, much of the terrible story of Ireland could also be the story of the continuing conflict between East Germany and Russia.

The best family vacation we ever took was on the sandy Adriatic coast of Croatia in Yugoslavia in the walled, mediaeval city of Dubrovnik built in the seventh century. Lord Byron called the city "the pearl of the Adriatic." In days past, the poets of the world identified many of their favorite places as "pearls."

The area surrounding Dubrovnik is permeated with ancient history: Richard the Lion Hearted was shipwrecked on an island a few hundred meters offshore in the Adriatic, and a hundred miles north in Split are the sprawling ruins of Roman Emperor Diocletian's retirement palace, built in the fourth century with accommodations for thousands. The walls of current houses are often the remaining, standing walls of Diocletian's vast palace.

The stolid, dour communist government functionaries who controlled our Dubrovnik hotel knew they themselves could not attract cash-laden tourists to the hotels, restaurants, and casinos so most employees who faced the public were effervescent Italians.

We fed the children their dinners early and then dressed and went downstairs to dine and put a few coins in play in the casino. The children were willing to be left alone in their room if we allowed them to jump on the bed, sleep with their dog, and order a before-bedtime snack of ice cream from room service. The wide sandy beaches provided them an unlimited daytime playground.

Our bills, when paid in dollars, were astonishingly modest: twenty dollars per night for two rooms and meals for four people in a top-of-the-line hotel; three cents for a cup of iced lemonade from a street vendor; and a few pocket coins for a tavern drink.

The poverty of the Yugoslavian people was evident on country roads. Rural girls walked barefoot to villages while carrying their shoes. When they arrived in town, they put on their shoes so they wouldn't seem so poor and rustic.

It appeared that in the countryside and villages, Muslims, Orthodox Christians, and Roman Catholics lived side-by-side in harmony; they built their churches and mosques on the same streets and they spoke different languages and dialects that they wrote in different alphabets (Latin,

Cyrillic, and Arabic.) They socialized and traded in the same public places and they intermarried. Later in the 1990s wars of genocide, this illusion of compatibility proved to be utterly false; thousands were killed. Ancient Dubrovnik was substantially damaged by shelling during the tragic war that divided the nation into six countries according to their many ethnic, religious, political, and linguistic parts. It was a time to settle differences that had been festering for more than a thousand years.

Periodically, John Deere's overseas employees were allowed to take home leave with family transportation costs absorbed on expense accounts.

On our first home leave we deviated from the direct flight path between Frankfurt and Chicago. We spent a week in the Virgin Islands in the Caribbean with Rita's childhood friends who were permanent residents. At two AM, during our ocean-crossing flight, we landed in the Azores to refuel. I stepped off our Avianca Airlines plane to stretch and look into the purest night sky imaginable while Rita and the children slept on the plane. I never forgot the dramatic sight into the window of heaven and maybe even eternity.

Our hosts lived in a house at the peak of a mountain with a view over the jungle to the Atlantic Ocean on one side and on the other side a view over the capital, Charlotte Amalie, to the Caribbean Sea. While sitting on the porch with our sunset rum drinks looking down the mountain to the harbor, we had the illusion that we could reach out through the evening tropical air and pick up the ships in the harbor—including the anchored aircraft carrier, Franklin D. Roosevelt—between our thumb and forefinger.

The motorists of the Virgin Islands drive on the left side of the road as a holdover from the days before World War I when the islands were owned by Denmark.

On the Atlantic side was pristine and sparsely used Magens Bay where we spent many hours swimming. Our three-old-son, John, found a seashell on the beach. He proudly told Rita he found a star that had fallen from heaven.

We then went on to Illinois and South Dakota to visit our families; I spent a few days working in my old office so that when I moved back to the US, I would still be remembered.

One Easter holiday Rita, Kathy, and John traveled to the US while I stayed in Europe. Lufthansa Airline employees made the trip as easy as possible for families with children. They arranged cars to pick up families at the exit ramp and drive them to the next-flight ramp. This, long before the age of hyper airport security examinations.

When they arrived in Rock Island, Kathy was dressed in a dirndl dress and John in lederhosen and a green felt hat with a feather, the traditional folk costumes of Bavaria. Rita's father never tired of talking about them stepping off the plane looking like the von Trapp children and Julie Andrews skipping through the alpine meadows in "The Sound of Music."

On the day after the long Easter weekend I had business in Madrid. Not wanting to be alone in cold, damp Germany, I left Heidelberg early and stopped over on the resort island of Palma de Majorca in the Mediterranean for two days. The flight stewardesses were in a dither because Freddy Quinn was aboard in the company of a tall blond. "Freddy"—as he was universally known—was the German version of Frank Sinatra and a national heartthrob in German-speaking countries. Freddy sang simple songs of the sea and rootless wandering in faraway lands.

Early the next morning I walked around the boat basin near my hotel to gawk at the sailboats and yachts. I was drawn to one boat because its sound system was blaring current Freddy songs. I noticed the person preparing the boat for the day's sail was Freddy himself. His blond companion soon bounded up the stairs from below turned out in crisp white sailing clothes with her hair flowing in the wind. Freddy nodded to her and formally shook her hand. I was amused at the irony of him having spent the night with her and then the next day treating her with the formality normally reserved for greeting a queen in a receiving line.

At the end of a weekend trip to Belgium, I left Rita, Kathy, and John with our red VW car to drive home to Heidelberg while I took a plane to Stockholm where I had business on Monday morning. Our quality-challenged car broke down along the road home in a torrential rain storm. An elderly Dutch couple stopped to offer help when they saw Rita and the children in distress. The husband drove Rita to a nearby town and found a mechanic while his wife "babysat" the children. We never stopped thinking well of the Dutch after this kindness.

On a quiet, snowy December evening, I drove with three German colleagues through the Belgian town of Bastogne and the surrounding snow- and ice-laden pine forests. We were scheduled to visit a competitor's combine factory the next day in Bruges. I knew the dreadful history of the famous World War II Battle of the Bulge, centered in Bastogne, where an American army was surrounded by the Nazis in their doomed, last gasp military push against the Western Allies. I knew of the great loss of life and several outright massacres of American prisoners. As we drove through Bastogne in the dark, I closed my eyes and imagined I could see and hear the raging battle between the German and American armies under the watchful eye of Ares, the Olympian god of war. I wondered if my German colleagues would comment on the famous and terrible battle—they did not. The Battle of the Bulge used up the last effective strength of the Nazis.

Unfortunately, Belgium was also the tramping grounds for foreign invaders on other occasions. In World War I, the British and the Germans duked it out in Belgian trenches like witless punch-drunk boxers.

We visited a World War I British cemetery in Flanders where a youthful generation of English soldiers was resting for all eternity. A surprising percent of the graves were for Irish mercenaries; their home counties in Ireland were carved on their tombstones.

Nearby were a simulated trench and cave complete with sound effects of machine guns and artillery barrages. Many of the German shells had contained asphyxiating chlorine and mustard gases that seeped into the trenches and caves making them crypts for thousands of hapless soldiers. The realism was uncanny and unsettling.

It was not possible to depart from the sad monuments in the solitary cemetery standing on foreign soil without recalling the haunting closing lines of John McCrae's poem written about the terrible war:

In Flanders Fields

The torch; be yours to hold it high
If ye break faith with us who die
We shall not sleep, though poppies grow
In Flanders field"

Rita could recite the entire poem from memory.

The brooding memorials and haunting poem were meant to be a warning to never again engage in the senseless futility of trench warfare. Indeed, trench warfare was seldom practiced again; better methods were soon developed to more efficiently and barbarically kill people. In less than twenty years the Nazis indoctrinated themselves on the wacko political and social propositions advocated in Hitler's ink-curdling diatribe, *Mein Kampf* (My Struggle), refitted their armies, rewrote the manuals on warfare, and let loose their hell hounds to become the scourge of much of Europe.

When I first traveled in Europe, I was often embarrassed at the ill-mannered behavior of some of my fellow Americans: dining in top-rated restaurants dressed in "clean-out-the-garage" clothes, asking for prices in "real money," and brusquely getting to the point in conversations and meetings at the expense of preliminary social etiquette.

I was less apologetic about Americans later when I saw the behavior of some Europeans when they traveled in foreign countries: intoxicated Germans complaining in restaurants about the unavailability of their favorite wursts or wines, Italians belligerently refusing to allow others to pass when they clogged up a walkway, and smug Swiss students arrogantly telling others what was wrong with their culture and governments.

We never lost our "deep urge to see the world, like the urge that brings up a worm in an Irish bog to see the moon when it's full."

After four years of European living, we would not claim that our comfortable travels rivaled the arduous trek of Marco Polo to Asia or the harrowing odysseys of Homer throughout the classical Mediterranean world, but we could say we traveled up to the limits of my vacation time and our budget.

John, Kathy, and Rita on the Adriatic Coast

Little Red Riding Hood House
Oberammergau, Bavaria

CHAPTER 14

CAREER PROGRESSION

*Far and away the best prize that life offers
is the chance to work hard at work worth doing.*
—Theodore Roosevelt

Frank Lyons at Engineering Drafting Board
John Deere—1959

When I was sixteen, my older brother received a letter and brochure from the South Dakota School of Mines and Technology, an engineering, mining, chemistry, physics, mathematics, and geology college in the Black Hills, inviting him to enroll. But he wanted more excitement in his life than further studying in a school; in a few days—unbeknownst to our parents—he enlisted in the army and spent the next two years living in the "excitement" of a remote Korean mudflat.

When I read the college brochure, I related engineering to my interest in being the tinkerer, mechanic, carpenter, and maintenance person on our South Dakota farm. On the spot, I decided that engineering was the logical next step for me; I would attend the School of Mines and become a mechanical engineer. I never wavered from this decision except for a brief time (about ten minutes) when I wanted to be a physicist. I soon found the physics department would need to significantly lower its required admittance standards if it had to accommodate me.

Two years later, after graduating from high school, I enrolled in the South Dakota School of Mines. I found I was ill-prepared for the demanding mathematics, chemistry, physics, and engineering classes. My mother, a teacher, had stressed studying Latin and English and promoted a liberal arts education at the expense of mathematics and science. It took me two years to catch up with courses that I missed in high school. But I caught up and graduated with my class.

My parents, who also had the education of six other children to consider, paid my tuition ($600 per year). I slung hash, waited tables in a bar, painted houses, worked as a surveyor, and tended gardens to pay for my room and board, transportation, and beer drinking.

When I graduated, engineering jobs were plentiful and employment offers were numerous. It was an exciting time.

I visited several companies and was offered jobs at DuPont, Gates Rubber, Honeywell, Oliver (Farm Equipment), and Fairbanks Morse. I accepted the offer from Fairbanks Morse in Beloit, Wisconsin for a salary of $375 per month.

After a year of working as an engineering trainee for Fairbanks Morse, a manufacturer of large industrial equipment (locomotives, pumps, large diesel engines, compressors, and electric motors), I still was at sea on what I specifically wanted to do with my career or what my engineering strengths were.

For the moment, the decision was made for me; I was drafted into the army because of the ongoing Korean War. The situation in divided Korea recalled a similar condition in Germany with the Russian military forces controlling one sector and the US and her allies another.

I was ordered to the Army Chemical Center near Baltimore to become part of a group of engineers, mathematicians, chemists, physicists, biologists, architects, and scientists established to utilize the talents of technically educated draftees.

My work assignment was to write repair parts manuals for tank flame throwers. I was assigned to work as the only GI in a federal civil service group. Much of my time was, in reality, "free time" because of the unchallenging requirements of the assignment.

To fully utilize my energy and occupy my spare time, I set up a variety of mini-entrepreneurial activities: painting houses, designing and building furniture and cabinets, selling wood working tools and wood products, and managing the post recreation craft shop nights and weekends (a paid job). Prior to my discharge two years later, I had banked my entire corporal's pay—$125 per month. While in the army, I lived well on my entrepreneurial earnings.

Fortunately, the Korean War ended a few months after I was drafted; I did not need to risk my life in combat.

My army tour was a time of personal growth. I had the opportunity to compare the staid Midwest culture to the more complex and worldly culture of the east coast. I also learned that people from different areas of the US were mutually clueless about each other. For example, as I was about to be discharged from the army, I bought a new suit for my new civilian job from a store clerk in Baltimore. When she asked where I was from, I said, "South Dakota." She responded, "But you don't have a southern accent!"

GIs from other regions of the country had to learn a new vocabulary and dialect when they moved to Maryland: soda (pop); far (fire); awl (oil); goen downie-ocean (going down to the Atlantic beach); Balamer, Merlin (Baltimore, Maryland), and Napolis (Annapolis), home of the state gubmit (government.)

In old Baltimore neighborhoods people are universally addressed as "hon." The Pope was welcomed at a later time for his visit to Baltimore with a banner across busy Charles Street proclaiming, "The Pope's Coming, Hon!"

Residing in Baltimore was like living in a comfortable boarding house with reasonable tolerance for many races, ethnicities, and creeds and universal agreement that seafood from the Chesapeake Bay is worth swooning over, especially steamed crabs eaten raccoon-fashion at newspaper-covered tables (to Midwesterners it's more like eating giant boiled grasshoppers).

The gentry and blue-collar class lived together in comfortable harmony and with universal contempt for outsiders who left the "s" off "John" when speaking of venerable Johns Hopkins University. The hallmark of Baltimore was its blocks of rowhouses with milky white marble steps that were scrubbed to radiance each morning.

The John Deere company made an engineer-recruiting visit to the Army Chemical Center when I was nearing discharge from the army, and I subsequently traveled to Moline, Illinois for a job interview in the corporate manufacturing engineering department. The job seemed to be in line with my career aspirations. I understood the company's farm equipment products and I could see how I could learn the "nitty-gritty" of my engineering profession while working for a company that made fundamental and worthwhile products. I did not want to work for a company that made products such as lethal bombs, tobacco products, junk food, DDT, or hula hoops. I accepted the John Deere job offer for a salary of $400 per month.

I left Baltimore in my paid-for green 1949 Oldsmobile sedan—commonly called "The Green Machine"—with all of my possessions in the trunk, a bank account of $1500, and no debts. I drove to Moline, rented a room for $8 per week with a shared bath and a telephone down the hall, and went to work the next day.

I settled down the next several years learning to be a design engineer for iron foundry equipment under the guidance of first-class engineers and managers. I still had spare time and lots of energy, so I worked evenings and weekends on the side providing engineering services to other local foundries. Although I became functionally competent as a design engineer, it was obvious to me that I would never be a Thomas Edison, Henry Ford, or Wright brother. I searched for ways to broaden my professional skills by enrolling in local college night courses. I registered for courses on philosophy and accounting but soon discontinued them because of extensive work travel.

Although the engineering work at John Deere was challenging and satisfying, I decided I wanted to move into a management role. When I was offered the opportunity to move to Germany as the project manager for building an iron foundry, it was the first step in that direction. The new assignment was a fast-learning experience. I soon realized that working in management took substantial communication and political skills.

I found out that I was a decent communicator and was comfortable talking to most people at any level of management. I was also seldom at a loss when discussing non-engineering subjects. However, it took a long time to learn the political skills required for management. Politics and people relationships did not follow the logical precision and clarity that I knew from studying mathematics and engineering.

I gradually learned that I did not need to master all of the engineering activities that I managed. It soon became obvious that it was better to depend on the technical expertise of other reliable engineers.

I was blessed with competent managers and job coaches for most of my career, although I was occasionally impeded with a few less-capable bosses—but that too became part of my learning experience.

During the four years that I worked in Germany and throughout Europe, I built a broad and valuable professional experience base that I could draw on for the rest of my life—two more decades working for John Deere; a decade as owner of Emerald Associates Inc., a consulting company; and as a volunteer for SCORE, a small business advisory group.

I was always interested in writing. After retirement, I turned to writing books and occasional op-ed articles for newspapers. *Heidelberg Days* is my fourth book.

When I go into the far turn of life and enter the next world, I hope I am typing at my computer and looking at a nearly completed book on the screen. And I dream that after my permanent departure from earth the waiting literary public will go on for years speculating on what brilliant ending I had in mind for my magnum opus.

First Employer—Fairbanks Morse & Co.
Heavy Equipment Manufacturer—Beloit, Wisconsin

Frank—Korean War Draftee—1955

Army Chemical Corp Insignia

Baltimore Row Houses
Daily White Marble Step Scrubbing Ritual

Famous Two-Cylinder John Deere Tractor

CHAPTER 15

GOING HOME

*Shod with wings is the horse of him who rides
On a spring day the road that leads to home.*
—Bai Juyi (825 BC)

*Breathes there the man, with soul so dead,
Who never to himself hath said,
This is my own, my native land!
Whose heart hath ne'er within him burn'd,
As home his footsteps he hath turn'd
From wandering on a foreign strand.*
—Edward Everett Hale

**Sailing for Home
Genoa to New York**

After the Mannheim foundry project was completed, I worked for a year in the John Deere regional headquarters in Heidelberg on projects in Spain, France, and Germany. When most of the company's large capital investment projects in Europe were finished, the need for my presence work in Europe ended, but other significant capital investments were planned and underway in the US. It was time for my family and me to pack up and return home.

We departed from Heidelberg in late 1967 to return to the "land of the round door knobs." (Germans used lever-type door handles.)

We left with mixed feelings. On a personal level, Rita and I would have preferred to continue living in Heidelberg for a while longer—especially Rita. When I told her of our transfer home, she recalled the opening line of a favorite poem, "The clock of life is wound but once." She added, "The best segment of time allotted to me from my clock winding was the four golden years of living in Heidelberg."

For our children, it was time to return home. We had seen other American children grow to adulthood in foreign lands without a feeling of being anchored to any nationality or country. When they became adults, they would be neither fish nor fowl.

For me it was time to reconnect professionally. Rapid changes were being made within John Deere and with technology. I did not understand all of them, and I needed to become a part of them to move forward with my career development.

Kathy had lived nearly half her life outside the US; John, three-quarters of his life. The US was a foreign land to them. Although we did not realize it at the time, Rita and I also came home as people quite different from the two Midwesterners who apprehensively boarded Lufthansa Airlines in Chicago four years earlier.

There had been a sea change in the cultural and political climate in the US during the four years that we lived away.

It was not easy to understand and accept all of the changes. We never would accept some of them—especially those stridently championed by flamboyant, uncivil, and disrespectful young people who lived off society and the hard, sober work of others without contributing a whit to it. We were repelled by graffiti in subways and on walls and railroad cars that proclaimed: Make love. Resist all authority. If it feels good, do it.

The list of significant events that occurred when we lived away was long.

Between 1962 and 1965 Pope John XXXIII convened a council of the Catholic Church hierarchy to "work on" Vatican II. The outcome was a major updating of centuries-old, outdated and rigid church practices. One of the major benefits was to draw all of the Christian faiths closer together as well as to connect to many non-Christian faiths. It was a shot in the arm to those who were drawing away from religion.

News broadcasters and journalists continued to report on the Cold War in Europe, but the more urgent reporting was switching to the escalating, shooting, and killing war in Southeast Asia and the violent anti-Vietnam war protests in the US. Even though President Johnson and General Westmorland announced the US was winning the war according to their scorecards, it was a pipe dream. Their criteria were not relevant for the kind of war being waged by the determined Vietnam enemy that fought from dark tunnels and the green shadowy forests.

The war was a continuing nightmare of bad political and military judgments. The patriotism and support for earlier US wars nearly vanished for many young people who rioted, moved to Canada to avoid the draft, defiled the flag, disrespected all things military, protested, sabotaged, drugged themselves, shirked, rebelled, forced the end of military training on many university campuses, and lost pride in being American.

The cost of the war was astronomical. It forced President Nixon to unilaterally abandon the long-standing fixed international exchange rates. The value of the dollar against other currencies plummeted and annual inflation zoomed up well over ten percent.

Jane Fonda's active opposition to the war and support of North Vietnam earned her the name, "Hanoi Jane." She characterized the US political and military leaders as war criminals and the returning POWs as liars who sought battlefield experience to beef up their career resumes.

When the North Vietnamese military captured and imprisoned US soldiers, sailors, and airmen, they did not follow the constraints specified in the Geneva Convention. When they abused their prisoners, they felt they were exacting a just punishment for indiscriminate bombings and massive use of Agent Orange (plant defoliant and herbicide) by the US.

Many sincere, honorable Americans abandoned faith in their government and supported the escalating demonstrations against US participation in the Vietnam War.

When veterans returned home, they were often disrespected and insulted. They thought they had honorably answered their call to duty, but were denied their just patriotic parades.

Having seen the patriotism and clarity of purpose in America during World War II when I was a boy, and to a lesser extent in the Korean War when I was a soldier, it took me a long time and a profound change in my attitude to conclude and accept that the Vietnam War was a blunder.

I could not believe that our well-educated, well-informed government leaders allowed the US to be sucked into the conflict. The ill-fated war was causing many young American people to withdraw from society and lose respect for older people who did not see the world as they saw it.

Rita arrived at an antiwar position sooner than I. She was enormously distressed that our young men in the prime of life were being killed or incapacitated for such a dubious purpose. She was brought to tears by a sad verse from an old Irish antiwar song that she thought expressed her viewpoint on the Vietnam War:

Johnnie, I Hardly Knew Ye

Where are your legs that used to run, hurroo, hurroo
Where are your legs that used to run, hurroo, hurroo
Where are your legs that used to run
When you went to carry a gun
Indeed your dancing days are done
Oh Johnny, I hardly knew ye.

The divisive Vietnam War was a malignant growth that was ripping the country apart. It would cause President Johnson to withdraw from the political stage as a presidential candidate when he realized he could not find an honorable way to end the war. He dreaded that he might be branded as the first US President to lose a war. He hoped he would be remembered instead for appointing Thurgood Marshall, the first black, to the Supreme Court; his Great Society programs, Medicare and Medicaid; and his support for Civil Rights. (He bashed the Ku Klux Klan for their racism by calling them, "A hooded society of bigots.")

Johnson limped out of Washington back to a life of tranquility and reflection on his small Pedernales River ranch in the Texas Hill Country. Things in Washington and Vietnam would get a lot worse after he left.

Mao Tse Tung launched his Cultural Revolution in China while we still lived in Germany. This was after the catastrophic failure of his "Great Leap Forward." The rules for governing in the new "Cultural Revolution" were set forth in a dopey tract commonly called *Mao's Little Red Book*. The Chinese citizens endured starvation, forced relocation, slavery, murder, assassinations, and mind-numbing reeducation according to the model developed earlier by Stalin in the Ukraine and Siberia. The Cultural Revolution dumped a generation of Chinese citizens through a trap door into a life of ignorance, misery, harshness, squalor, and hopelessness seldom seen since the Dark Ages in Europe.

Mao could do whatever he wanted; he now had his own A-bomb and no viable adversaries. China, with twenty percent of the world population, lay like a wounded dragon beside the road in the 1960s. But those with acute strategic vision knew sometime it would awake, bind its wounds, recall thousands of years of past glory and achievements in China, and again become a consequential world force.

Women in the US were freed from many of the past constraints on their gender. They began to demand a better future: equal wages, better jobs, leadership roles in business and the government, more education, independent lifestyles, and shared family-raising responsibilities. It would be a long road for them to travel.

Birth control pills revolutionized the biological lifestyle of women and advanced female liberation. Sexual liberation caused profound changes.

In Houston, Dr. Denton Cooley made the first implantation of an artificial heart. For this trail-blazing achievement and other medical procedure developments, Cooley became a legend.

Little-known Warren Buffet gained control of Berkshire-Hathaway and sold its stock for $18 per share. By 2008, the stock would be worth $150,000. Buffet and selected others would rapidly accumulate sky-high fortunes that had not been seen since the days of the Wall Street robber barons of the late 1800s. The skewing of wealth to the privileged few at the top and subsistence living for many at the bottom would remain an unresolved issue for many decades.

Rock n' roll music swamped the airwaves led by the stratospheric popularity of the mop-haired Beatles. Their music was a perfect fit with the youth culture and lifestyle of the 1960s.

When Walt Disney died in 1966, immortal Mickey Mouse, Donald Duck, and Snow White and the seven dwarfs doffed their hats and mourned for their mortal creator. While entertaining the world, Disney also established the business model used later by Bill Gates, Steve Jobs, and others as he led his talented teams and set nearly impossible artistic and technical objectives for them.

Legendary, five-star General Douglas MacArthur "just faded away" as he promised in his farewell speech to Congress after Truman and the Joint Chiefs of Staff "dismissed" him from the army for disobedience to the orders of his commander in chief. When Truman later read MacArthur's maudlin speech to Congress, he called it, "A damned bunch of B.S."

In the racially segregated sections of the US, many profoundly objected to the civil rights movement. George Wallace, governor of Alabama, declared, "segregation today, segregation tomorrow, and segregation forever." (He later recanted these words.) Lester Maddox was photographed wielding an axe handle at blacks attempting to patronize his "whites-only" Pickrick Café. The photo helped him be elected governor of Georgia. A lengthy, and sometimes bloody, social revolution was underway to redress long-standing civil rights injustices.

The hippie movement—although reviled by many—was a voice for positive activism in some areas. It turned a needed spotlight on environmental issues, social injustice, questionable wars, and responsible energy consumption. The hippies thought they could positively change the world. But others regarded the hippie movement as irrational and uncivilized, believing the movement fostered an attitude of: Let's walk away from everything we ever knew and be as free as the birds in the air and the dogs and cats in the back alleys. It's OK to groom like mangy animals. Witless consumption of life-destroying drugs is alright. It's acceptable to treat human bodies like road meat. Freeloading on the back of society is the thing to do.

Dr. Timothy Leary, a spokesman for LSD drug users, was known for his catch phrase, "Turn on, tune in, and drop out."

But the hippie movement of the 1960s would run its course. After 1970, most young people became less concerned with changing the world and more anxious to find paying jobs.

For the first time, federal and state governments demanded that tobacco sellers provide conspicuous warnings about smoking health hazards. The Germans had identified the link between tobacco and lung cancer in the 1940s, but the information was soft-pedaled. Later the CEOs of four major tobacco companies sat in Congress like four wooden Pinocchios and read their identical lawyered-up statements denying any knowledge of harm from smoking tobacco. This in spite of what every farmhand and factory worker in the country already knew when they called their "ciggies" coffin nails. The "big tobacco" CEOs departed from the hearings with noticeably longer noses. None would ever be prosecuted for perjury.

Bobby Kennedy, the hyper-intense icon for liberal factions and a passionate voice for civil rights, was assassinated several months after Martin Luther King was shot. Parts of the country were literally in flames during riots and looting in more than 100 cities such as Detroit, where 43 people died and 2,550 buildings were burned or looted. The civil rights movement came to a full conflagration after years of smoldering.

Shortly after returning home from Germany, I traveled to the Detroit City Airport on a company plane; it was a white knuckle landing and takeoff since a few days earlier, rioters had shot at low-flying planes. When we were out of gunfire range, a wry colleague said, "I feel like a marine departing from Khe Sanh (Vietnam) on a helicopter."

For Rita and me, it was easy to accept gender equality, elimination of civil rights injustices, and better environmental laws. But it was not so easy to imagine raising our children in an atmosphere of lowered moral standards and seeming disregard for physical appearance and personal behavior in public.

Other less momentous things also happened in the US during our absence. "Swinging London" gave the US and the world the miniskirt, which became an early symbol for woman's liberation. New looks came into vogue: bouffant hairdos, long sideburns, Nehru jackets, bikinis, blue jeans for every occasion, and Afros. The Beatles sang "Strawberry Fields Forever" and Evel Knievel jumped his motorcycle over sixteen cars. Motorists paid thirty-three cents per gallon for gasoline.

Many of these happenings were game-changers and a few were passing fads. The "old days" were gone. The changes were welcomed by many, but for some of the old guard they were as unacceptable as it would have been for my grandfather to stop "saucering" his coffee, eating his food off the blade of his knife, and salting his food from a salt cellar.

My family and I were given much during the four years that we lived away from the US. We learned to live in a new culture. But when we returned home, the culture that we left behind in 1964 had changed. We had to adjust to the realities of the changed world and learn new ways and attitudes.

A half century later, at the time I wrote this book, most of the issues and problems that seemed intractable and unsolvable in 1968 have been resolved and many of the dreams have been realized.

West and East Germany were successfully and peacefully reunited. The Cold War ended with the speed of light partly because communist propaganda could no longer trump real-time television broadcasting from the noncommunist world. The dreaded atomic weapons that threatened Armageddon remain safely locked in Pandora's box; the risk of mutual destruction from the weapons prevented the nuclear arsenal-keepers from ever opening it. The domino theory—if one country falls to the communists, others will follow— proved to be the fallacious vision of Washington policy wonks. World communism and the Soviet Union crumbled like a decrepit, termite-ridden barn collapsing without fanfare in the middle of the night. For a couple of decades, at least, Russia seemed to lose the will to dominate the world and bludgeon her adversaries into submission. Reunited Germany became the stable political and economic linchpin of Europe. Germany kept her long-standing military ambitions for expanding in Europe in check, but ironically she came to substantially control much of the continent anyhow with her gigantic economic power and political stability. In the heavy industrial and energy generating zones of Germany, suffocating and lethal pollution were curbed—partly due to the confrontational activism of Greenpeace.

One of the epic events of the twentieth century was the grand experiment to introduce communism as the dominate political and economic force throughout the world. Although many in the noncommunist world thought communism would ultimately fail, they did not realize that when it did, the people raised in the all-controlling system would find it difficult to make the transition to freedom. Formerly subjugated people were ill pepared to determine their own destinies after lifetimes of control, propagandizing, deprivation, imprisonment, terror, limited education, and forced work under harsh conditions.

After the communist system failed, many people were anchorless and adrift. They fell back to old habits of waiting to be told what to do, making shoddy products, corruption, ignoring the voice of the marketplace, failing to take personal responsibility, and drinking too much. They were like people who were imprisoned from youth to old age and then released with the expectation that they would be able to live their lives in a free society. There would not be another economic miracle in Russian and her satellites as there was earlier in West Germany.

It seemed that the best option for the collapsed communist world was to adopt the structures of the West: democracy, capitalism, and freedom. But this was a nearly insurmountable challenge without the West's centuries of slowly built traditions, laws, trade agreements, ethics, work habits, and financial organizations. And what was to be done with obsolete plants, rampant pollution, dysfunctional market systems, and incompetent and corrupt leaders? And how should the long-cherished, dinosaur-like Leninist principles be buried? In Russia and her satellites, the heritage of an unworkable government, a junky economy, and the utter humiliation of her "great fall" would need to be borne for decades.

Alexis de Tocqueville, a French political thinker and historian, accurately foresaw the problem for Russia and her satellites more than a century earlier when he wrote, "The most dangerous time for a bad government is when it starts to reform itself."

During our stay in Germany in the mid-1960s and for several years thereafter, the establishment of John Deere as the dominant company in its field in Europe seemed for some to be a pipedream. But the company's senior management steadfastly stuck with its objectives. In the 1970s the European business started to contribute the company's financial success.

The European business continues to grow based on the lessons learned during the hard times on the 1960s.

Social and political viewpoints in Germany and America always differed from each other, but they have diverged further in the last half century.

Liberal viewpoints on social welfare and related subjects—medical care, vacation time, holidays, retirement, job security, work hours, maternity leave, and unemployment—have existed since prewar days in Germany and most of Europe. Europeans work three hundred fewer hours per year than Americans. To fire an employee in Europe is difficult and costly. To pay for the generous social welfare system, the Europeans tolerate sky-high graduated income taxes.

The Europeans know their costly welfare system retards economic growth, but they think it is better than the American way of "growth at all cost." They believe citizens deserve to be shielded from the economic ups and downs caused by the cyclical market place. Nye Bevan, a British labor leader, described market driven economics as being "something carried over from Neanderthal times."

The dyed-in-the-wool German attitudes on a welfare society are being put to the test in the 2000s. Because of dramatically declining European birth rates, there are not enough people to man the economy and pay for costly social services (health care and pensions) for the long-living elderly population.

Germans and many other Europeans are critical of Americans who work so hard for material acquisitions and then have little time left "to smell the roses." In Germany the welfare system also provides the roses. They generously fund operas, ballets, art galleries, and orchestras. More than a half million people in Germany are paid "artistic workers."

Since the Europeans have blurred the lines of nationalism through the unified European economic system and multination NATO, they fall short on decisiveness and action when crises occur.

While the divergence between the cultures of Germany—as well as most of Europe—and the US continues, Germany sees herself as a wise old man offering wisdom and counsel from a park bench. She ascribes her wisdom to her life of severe economic times between the two world wars, the barbaric excesses of World War II, and the half-century long, harrowing standoff with Russia during the Cold War. She sees America as the Lone Ranger naively galloping into town to shoot the bad guys, crack a few heads, and make things right.

Germany is ambivalent about her military role and defense budgets. With her per capita investment in her military being one-third that of the

US, she knows she cannot stand alone. Criticism of the vast US military capability is tricky. When there are no major threats on the horizon, it is easy for Germany to criticize the US high military budgets and advanced fighting capabilities.

During the Cold War, the threat of a major war was the dominant force that drove German foreign policy; Bonn was in lockstep with Washington out of necessity. Since communism was sucked away into a black hole and the elimination of the Russian military threat, Germany, and much of Europe, see events through different lenses. They now feel free to throw stones of criticism west across the Atlantic. Without the Cold War to necessitate a US/Western Europe alliance, Europe thinks she can now afford to openly criticize the US and go her separate way.

Rudyard Kipling aptly wrote about a comparable, peaceful time during the history of the British Empire when there was not a military threat and when her soldiers were not needed or respected:

Tommy

Oh it's Tommy this, an' Tommy that, an' "Tommy, go away";
But it's "Thank you, Mister Atkins", when the band begins to play,
The band begins to play, my boys, the band begins to play,
Oh it's "Thank you, Mister Atkins", when the band begins to play.

Serious German strategic thinkers know that someday "when the band begins to play" again in Europe, she will need a friendly big brother to help protect her. In the meantime, those who think in a smaller arena can afford to cast stones across the Atlantic Ocean towards the US. Although the US is the only superpower in the world today, other countries have the potential to ascend to prominence in coming decades and become German adversaries.

Most Germans were opposed to the US role in the Iraq war. They saw the US as a blundering, arrogant nation that bulled ahead with the war based on inadequate, as well as false, intelligence and little interest in the opinions of European NATO countries. The majority of Europeans have little confidence in the current leadership from Washington.

Germans cannot understand the US infatuation with the personal ownership of firearms; they think the attitudes from the days of the Wild West still prevail. Germans can own firearms for hunting and competitive shooting but with strict control. They believe they have a more enlightened way for legitimate gun ownership: training, psychological testing, and licensing. They are appalled at the senseless killing rampages in schools and public places in the US by psychologically disturbed people with virtual arsenals of legally acquired firearms and ammunition.

Until the early 2000s, the US followed a path in the opposite direction from Europe on most issues related to economics, social matters, self-reliance, gun control, market-driven forces, and the use of military force.

In 2014, at the time of this book writing, the US is in the throes of a ferocious, no-holds-barred national debate on whether the US should follow her old path: individualism, minimum taxes, minimum government, and market-driven economics. Or should she fundamentally expand the role of the federal government in the direction of the more liberal Europeans? The jury is still out as Congress and the White House deliberate.

Hoisting Anchor in Genoa

On Deck
Kathy, Rita, John, and Frank

The Fall of Saigon, Vietnam—1975

CHAPTER 16

WHAT CAME NEXT

Everybody has gone through something that has changed them in a way that they could never go back to the person they once were.
—kusandwizdom

The present is the food of the future.
—Edward Councel

John Deere Corporate Headquarters
Moline, Illinois

When we returned home to live again in the US, John Deere was embarking on a major worldwide expansion. New factories, foundries, warehouses, and offices were needed. John Deere was hiring additional experienced people to supplement its in-house staff for planning, engineering, and construction. The new people brought with them significantly different ways of conducting large-scale projects. I would need to understand the changes and adjust to them. It would take time—and an occasional toe stubbing.

I was appointed project manager for planning, designing, and building a new diesel engine factory in Waterloo, Iowa. The factory was planned to manufacture three hundred diesel engines per day in a million-square-foot facility. The investment cost was $500 million when converted to 2014 dollars.

Waterloo is surrounded by rich, endless corn and bean fields. John Deere tractors can be delivered to nearby farmers and working in the fields while they are still warm from the factory paint drying ovens.

After the project was well underway, the forecast sales of engines jumped and the country underwent a major spike in the inflation rate. It required considerable dexterity to react to the changes. The sales increase was welcome, but the factory redesign and the trip back to the board of directors for additional investment funds were challenges.

Later, I became the project manager for planning and building a combine assembly factory in Zweibrücken, Germany, located on the German/French border. The combine factory was planned to satisfy the widely varying needs of customers in many countries. Unique marketing requirements necessitated speed and agility.

Russian and Eastern European customers did not have leak-proof grain wagons or storage bins. Laborers stood on top of the combines to catch the harvested grain in burlap bags. This primitive practice had ended decades earlier in Western Europe and North America. Middle East customers needed to save as much straw as possible to use as the binder material for adobe bricks. This necessitated the special design of straw-catching wagons pulled behind the combines.

Zweibrücken was a small town in a rural setting. Across from the factory entrance sat a farmer's barn. The road between them was temporarily blocked at harvest time so the farmer could unload and store his fall turnip crop (used as animal feed). Everyone understood and tolerated the inconvenience of the road detour.

At the edge of the factory property stood an open meadow. Each evening a twenty-member herd of miniature deer came out to graze under the window of our project workroom. The deer were oblivious to the new factory that was about to reduce their habitat.

It was gratifying to work in a close relationship with farmers, rural life, and nature. It recalled to me my childhood on a South Dakota farm.

While working on the combine project, I visited my old neighborhood and house sixty miles away in Heidelberg. The house door was open because of rehabilitation work; I stepped in and was pleased to see that all of the original fine floors and woodwork were retained.

I had the opportunity during and after the engine project to work with and receive the backing of two supportive and encouraging executives.

Bob Chaney, who was my boss, previously ran a John Deere diesel engine factory, directed other significant factory operations, and was a US Navy Reserve skipper. His advice and example were invaluable to me. He later became a factory general manager.

Bill Van Sant, the Waterloo engine factory general manager and later the corporate vice president of engineering, and I worked hand-in-glove in a trusting and respectful alliance during the engine project. A few years later, he resigned to become the president of Cessna Aircraft Company.

Bob Chaney and Bill Van Sant were helpful to me in many ways for my professional development and career improvement.

After I was appointed manager of a division of the John Deere Engineering Department, I did less travelling. Because of a lifelong interest in antique British cars, I bought a 1950 Riley convertible and rebuilt it from top to bottom—a five-year project. After driving the car on nice summer days for many years, I sold it to an Oslo, Norway, car collector.

I also bought a 1935 Rolls Royce car. I partially completed its restoration when I again went on the road with the work of my newly founded company. I sold the car before completing its restoration.

Owning antique cars is like owning yachts; the two happiest days are the day of purchase and the day of sale.

For decades, we endlessly built additions, redecorated, modified, and refurnished our Rock Island house and garden. The original colonial house was designed by Rita's architect father when we were first married.

In the late 1970s and early 1980s, the agricultural industry went into a severe economic nosedive that lasted for several years. John Deere was one of the few farm equipment companies to survive. Even mighty competitor International Harvester went to the wall. When its large tractor factory in Rock Island closed, it was a crushing economic blow to the community. Further expansion within John Deere came to a temporary standstill. Going to work was no longer the pleasure it had always been.

The company made a generous early retirement offer to reduce employment. I accepted the offer after thirty-one years of an exciting and fulfilling career working for a company that provided products and services for the good of humanity.

As I sat in my office before retiring, I mused about the earlier uncertainties and risks relative to John Deere's decision to heavily invest in European markets in the 1960s. At that time, high risks existed: Did the company have the correct products and business model for Europe? Did it understand the markets? If Russia and communism won the Cold War in Europe, would John Deere's investments be confiscated? Could the large initial European financial losses continue and possibly overwhelm the entire company? Would the board of directors replace the top management if the financial losses went on too long? The risks were scary, but none of the most worrisome scenarios ever materialized. I ended my musing by thinking of my good fortune to have directly participated in a very small way in John Deere's European success.

I soon found that I was not ready for retirement. I started a consulting company, Emerald Associates Inc., which offered strategic manufacturing planning and other technical services to manufacturing firms. In several instances, we supplied temporary factory managers. Emerald prospered while providing services in the US, Canada, Mexico, Italy, and Czechoslovakia.

Emerald's work in a Czech tractor factory gave us an insight into a business built on communist principles. Even though the communist world had recently collapsed, the Russian way of doing business was too "institutionalized" to kill: shoddy quality, trashy products, corruption, and indifference to the voice of the market place. Some of the Czech-manufactured tractors were modified and bought by John Deere to have a low-price product to sell in Latin America. But the Czech company could not deny its heritage; the tractors were called "watermelon tractors"— green on the outside but red inside. The business arrangement with John Deere soon ended.

Some of the products manufactured by Emerald's clients were home appliances, helicopters, locomotives, textiles, sugar cane harvesters, agricultural and industrial equipment, computer equipment housings, steel, and reinforcing steel for concrete highways.

While I worked for John Deere, I observed that our hired consulting firms were usually in a feast or famine mode. In lean times they frantically grabbed any contracts they could to meet their payroll needs and to remain profitable. At Emerald we overcame this problem by hiring employees as "independent contractors" with the understanding that their employment would only last for the duration of the contracts in our order books. This was acceptable to our employees, who were recently retired engineers with pensions or who were still employed elsewhere. During Emerald's peak year we hired forty part-time, remarkably talented employees whose annual work time for Emerald varied from a few days to full time.

Although it was relatively easy for Emerald to provide strategic planning services to our clients based on our previous experiences, it was more difficult to learn the required additional skills: marketing, sales, administration, pricing, business laws, insurance, foreign business practices, and accounting. Marketing and sales were the most challenging. We soon learned that selling was mostly the art of listening to client needs, not talking about ourselves.

We had to learn to perform outside the safe and protective cocoon provided by our previous large corporate employers with their regiments of support personnel. Emerald was aided in its management decisions by the guidance and advice of an experienced advisory board.

Because of the broad domestic and international experiences of Emerald's employees, we could precisely match the appropriate project assignees to the client's job requirements. We could also assign people who could speak some of the languages of our clients—English, Spanish, and Italian.

We were able to compete with large international competitors. One of our most gratifying times was when a large client reversed its decision to order manufacturing consulting services from a world-renowned firm and instead favored Emerald with the order.

It was fascinating for us to work in industries that were new to us. While working in the Hughes Aircraft Division of McDonnell Douglas in Mesa, Arizona, we were surrounded by a sprawling campus-like factory that made the famous and lethal Apache helicopter—virtually a flying tank. Apaches are sold around the world, sometimes to the military of countries that were adversaries or even at war with each other. The Apache Longbow version can sight and simultaneously shoot its rockets to multiple, over-the-horizon targets. Working with defense companies that had to follow rigid Department of Defense rules was a challenge.

One of the most beautiful places where Emerald undertook a project was in northern Italy in the Lake District between Italy and Switzerland. The eating was legendary, the sightseeing was awesome, and weekend operatic performances were numerous. And the work for our client was rewarding.

Business cards of recent retirees frequently show their occupation as "consultant"—often really meaning "unemployed." Fortunately Emerald was able to attract meaningful client orders.

Years after our return to the US, our daughter Kathy became a teacher and later a paralegal and manager of the stockholder relations department of the Wrigley company in Chicago. She married Dr. David Tabak, her college boyfriend, and later became the administrative manager of his optometric practice. They have one adult son, Joe Tabak. Kathy now devotes most of her time to volunteer organizations in and around Barrington, the Chicago suburbs where she lives.

John became an investment advisor; he is a Merrill Lynch representative for institutional clients. He recently married Meghan Collins, and they live and work in San Francisco. John and Meghan devote a considerable part of their spare time, talent, and resources to charities that serve needy people.

Rita continued to be an exemplary mother, wife, teacher, and community "presence." She renewed her teaching license and taught high school part time for many years. She loved to banter with her teen-age students. Her subscription to "Mad Magazine" allowed her to keep abreast of the latest teen lingo and subjects of interest, much to the amusement of her pupils. She devoted a great deal of her time and considerable talents to leading a broad range of community volunteer activities: Saint Pius X Church Council, St. Vincent de Paul Society, Questers Antique Club, American Orchid Society, PEO, a quilting club, bridge clubs, a dinner club, and the Colonel Davenport House Foundation. And she always had time to comfort and advise anyone who needed cheering up.

The most profoundly difficult day of my life occurred after Emerald Associates had been in operation for three years. Rita was killed in an automobile accident.

My feelings about her death are best expressed through the words of ancient Chinese Emperor Wu-ti when he wrote of the death of his consort:

> The sound of her silk skirt has stopped.
> On the marble pavement dust grows.
> Her empty room is cold and still.
> Fallen leaves are piled against the doors.
> Longing for that lovely lady,
> How can I bring my aching heart to rest?

The work of Emerald was a blessing; it occupied my mind as I grieved for Rita and it gave me the strength to move on with my life.

After six years, Emerald was fully established and had surpassed its original business objectives. I felt no compelling reason to continue with the stress, travel, and long working hours. I sold the company and again retired.

All my life, I have been interested in writing. I now have the time to author and publish books. *Heidelberg Days* is my fourth publication.

I also devote part of my time to volunteering with SCORE, a small business advisory group of retired professionals and business owners that helps people start businesses or improve on-going businesses. This work provides the opportunity for staying up-to-date on technology and business practices in the rapidly changing world.

After Rita's death, I renewed an acquaintanceship with a friend, Jean Schramm Monier, from my army days in Baltimore. When I first met her, she was a biologist at the Army Chemical Center where she worked as a civilian researching alternative antidotes for lethal nerve gas (also called Sarin or G-gas.) She married my army barracks friend, Marcel Monier, who died a year before Rita. After Jean and I dated for some months, she resigned from her lifelong career as a college biology professor and in later years as the alumnae director for her college, College of Notre Dame of Maryland. We married in her college chapel, and she moved to my home in Rock Island, Illinois. She successfully made the transition to Midwest living after having resided in New York City as a child and then in Virginia, New Jersey, and Maryland.

As my "wound-only-once" clock of life ticks onward, I am comforted when I read the refrain in a W.B. Yeats' poem, "Those Dancing Days Are Gone." Yeats wrote of an aging man recalling his pleasant younger days while gracefully accepting and enjoying his sunset years:

> I carry the sun in a golden cup.
> The moon in a silver bag.

John Deere Engine Works
Waterloo, Iowa

John Deere Engine Works Office
Waterloo, Iowa

John Deere Combine Assembly Line
Zweibrücken, Germany

John Lyons and Kathy (Lyons) Tabak

Jean Monier Lyons

Restored 1950 Riley

Office Sign

Emerald's Most Valued Client

An Emerald Client
Electro-Motive Diesel

BIBLIOGRAPHY

Applebaum, Anne, *Gulag*
Doubleday, 2003

Applebaum, Anne, *Iron Curtain*
Doubleday, 2012

Arendt, Hannah, *Eichmann in Jerusalem: A Report on the Banality of Evil*
Penguin Classics, 2006

Bacque, James, *Crimes and Mercies*
Little Brown and Company, 1997

Bailey, George, *Germans*
The Free Press, 1991

Bessel, Richard, *German 1945*
Harper Perennial, 2010

Brohl, Wayne G., *John Deere's Company*
Doubleday and Company, 1984

Dolot, Miron, *Execution by Hunger: The Hidden Holocaust*
W.W. Norton and Company, 1965

de Zayas, Alfred Maurice, *A Terrible Rage*
Saint Martin's Press, 1986

Fritsch-Bournazel, Renate, *Confronting the German Question*
Berg Publishing, 1986

Fulbrook, Mary, *Interpretation of the Two Germanys*
St Martin's Press, 2000

Gray, William Glenn, *Germany's Cold War*
University of North Carolina Press, 2003

Judt, Tony, *Postwar: A History of Europe since 1945*
Penguin Books, 2005

Mierzejewski, Alfred C., *Ludwig Erhard*
University of North Carolina Press, 2004

McAdams, A. James, *Germany Divided*
Princeton University Press, 1993

MacDonogh, Giles, *After the Reich*
Basic Books, 2007

Neider, Charles (editor), *The Autobiography of Mark Twain—
100 Anniversary Edition*
Harper Collins, 1999

O'Connor, Anne-Marie, *The Lady in Gold*
Random House, 2012

Shirer, William, *Rise and Fall of the Third Reich*
Simon and Schuster, 1960

Taylor, Frederich, *Exercising Hitler*
Bloomsbury Publishing, 2011

Turner, Henry Ashby Jr., *Germany from Partition to Reunification*
Yale University Press, 1991

Uris, Leon, *Armageddon*
Doubleday & Co., Inc., 1964

Von Oechelhaeuser, Adolf, *Castle of Heidelberg*
Dr. Johannes Hörning Heidelberg, Printer and Publisher, 1956

Zusak, Markus, *The Book Thief*
Alfred A. Knopf, 2005

PHOTOGRAPHIC CREDITS

The photographs in this book are reproduced by permission and courtesy of the following:

Book Cover—Dreamstime

Chapter 1—Moving to Germany
- Lufthansa Plane—Internet
- Map of Heidelberg, Mannheim, and Handschusheim—Wikipedia
- Company Name in Transition—The Plowshare (Issue #28)
- President Kennedy in Dallas—CBS News

Chapter 2—Heidelberg
- Panorama of Heidelberg—Dreamstime
- Panorama of Heidelberg—Dreamstime
- Heidelberg Castle— Dreamstime
- Philosophers Way—unknown
- Old Bridge—Dreamstime
- Heidelberg City Map—unknown

Chapter 3—Overseas Expansion
- Hay Wagon—Wikipedia
- Competitor Logos—Wikipedia
- Old John Deere Logo—Internet
- Original John Deere Plow—Internet

Chapter 4—Living in Germany
- Lyons Home—Lyons Files
- Rita and Dog—Lyons Files
- Handschuhsheim Logo—Internet
- Volkswagen—Lyons Files
- Birthday Party—Lyons Files
- Chimney Sweep—Wikipedia
- Family Portrait—Lyons Files
- Children with Pretzels—Lyons Files

Chapter 5—The German People
- Pandora's Box—Wikipedia
- Nazi Rally—*Life* Magazine
- The Four Horsemen of the Apocalypse—Wikipedia

Chapter 6—The Konrad Adenauer Era
- Adenauer—Wikipedia
- Berlin Ruins—Wikipedia
- Map of Postwar Berlin—Wikipedia
- Map of Postwar Europe—Internet
- Lübke, McCoy, and Adenauer—Wikipedia
- Eisenhower and Adenauer—Internet

Chapter 7—Building an Iron Foundry
- Iron Molders—Stained Glass Window—Burrell Collection, Stephan Adams
- Iron Casting—Wikipedia
- Cast Iron Block—Wikipedia

Chapter 8—The Ludwig Erhard Era
- Erhard—Google Images
- Erhard and Johnson—Wikipedia
- McCloy and Erhard—American Council on Germany

Chapter 9—The Looming Bear to the East
- Bear with Stalin in Mouth—Unknown
- Yalta Conference—PBS
- Red Army Entering Berlin—Wikipedia
- Surrender at Stalingrad—NKVD Files

Chapter 10—Postwar West Germany
- Back to Normal 1963—Len Marriott
- Minicar—Wikipedia
- Reclaiming Bricks from Rubble—Wikipedia

Chapter 11 Postwar East Germany
- Kennedy Looking Over Wall—Google Images
- Berlin Airlift—Google Images
- Barbed Wire Fence—Google Images

Chapter 12—Postwar Nightmare
- Buchenwald Concentration Camp—Wikipedia

- Nuremberg Trials—Google Images
- Berlin Holocaust Memorial—Wikipedia

Chapter 13—Personal Travels
- Dubrovnik—Google Images
- Adriatic Coast, Rita, Kathy, and John—Lyons Files
- Little Red Riding Hood House—Pinterest

Chapter 14—Career Development
- Frank Lyons at Drafting Board—Lyons Files
- Fairbanks Morse Engine—Internet
- Army Chemical Center Insignia—Wikipedia
- Frank Lyons in Uniform—Lyons Files
- Baltimore Marble Steps—A. Aubrey Bodine
- John Deere Tractor—Internet

Chapter 15—Going Home
- Boarding Michelangelo—Lyons Files
- Hoisting Anchor—Lyons Files
- Family on Deck of Michelangelo—Lyons Files
- Helicopter Evacuating Saigon—Google Images

Chapter 16—What Next?
- Deere and Co. World Headquarters—The Garden and Landscape Guide
- Emerald Associates Inc. Office Sign—Lyons Files
- John and Kathy Lyons—Lyons Files
- Restored Riley—Lyons Files
- John Deere Engine Works—Deere & Co. Files
- John Deere Engine Works Entry—Deere & Co. Files
- Combine Assembly Factory—Wikipedia
- Jean Monier Lyons—Monier Files

Other Books by Author—Lyons Files

St Vincent de Paul Logo—Internet

ACKNOWLEDGEMENTS

There are many fingerprints besides mine on *Heidelberg Days*.

My wife Jean (Monier) Lyons was my constant sounding board for discussing words, expressions, and clarity of meaning. She then read the entire manuscript to me so I could listen for the sound and rhythm of the words.

My daughter, Kathy (Lyons) Tabak, who lived with us as a girl in Heidelberg, brought to my attention events from her childhood memories. She then read and commented—with penetrating eyes—on the manuscript.

Although my son, John Lyons, was too young to remember much from living as a young boy in Heidelberg, he later lived for a time as a university student in Austria and Switzerland, where he learned a great deal about the German culture and language. And he remembered a lifetime of our family talking of our Heidelberg days. He read the manuscript and added his perspective.

My brother, Bob Lyons, has spent a lifetime studying and writing. He read the manuscript and made useful comments.

Cal Peterson, a John Deere executive who lived in Heidelberg during the late 1960s and 1970s, provided useful suggestions for the book.

Dale Whiteside worked in Germany as a German/English interpreter while in the US Army. He offered numerous insights on the German language and culture.

Catherine Butterworth, a university student studying English, ably edited the manuscript.

Connie Richardson, a professional editor, commented on the manuscript and prepared the book format for submission to the publisher.

Bob Chaney, a friend for many years, generously provided a house, palm tree shade, and warm soothing Caribbean breezes in the Yucatan of Mexico where I wrote much of this book.

I owe much to these and other people for their help in making *Heidelberg Days* a reality.

The Die Is Cast
A Novel About Corporate Corruption

by Frank Lyons

Available on Amazon

South Dakota Days
A History of the Rural Midwest
in the 1930s and 1940s

by Frank Lyons

Available on Amazon

ROYALTIES to ST. VINCENT de PAUL SOCIETY

I was hungry and you gave me food, I was thirsty and you gave me something to drink, I was a stranger and you welcomed me, I was naked and you gave me clothing, I was sick and you took care of me, I was in prison and you visited me.
—Matthew 25: 35–36

In recollection of the millions of people who suffered hunger, starvation, and other deprivations in Europe during World War II, the royalties for *Heidelberg Days* will be donated to the St. Vincent de Paul Society, which was founded in France in the 1600s to serve the poor and disadvantaged and later expanded to more than one hundred countries around the world.

St Vincent de Paul Society programs include food pantries, dining halls, home visits, housing assistance, disaster relief, job training and placement, clothing, transportation, utility payments, and care and medicine for the elderly. In the US, the society serves 14 million needy and suffering people annually.

FRANK LYONS understands West Germany from living there with his family in the 1960s and extensive travel and reading since. After a long career as an engineering executive of a Fortune 500 company and the founder and president of an international manufacturing consulting company, he turned to writing. He lives on the Mississippi River in Rock Island, Illinois, where he continues to write.